CW01467858

We're
Shiftin'

To Ros
Many thanks for your help in putting my
stories together. Without your assistance this
book would never have been completed.

We're Shiftin'

A Gloucestershire Childhood

Richard Pottinger

BREWIN BOOKS

BREWIN BOOKS
56 Alcester Road,
Studley,
Warwickshire,
B80 7LG
www.brewinbooks.com

Published by Brewin Books 2018

© Richard Pottinger, 2018

The author has asserted his rights in accordance with the
Copyright, Designs and Patents Act 1988 to be
identified as the author of this work.

All rights reserved. No part of this publication may be
reproduced, stored in a retrieval system, or transmitted in
any form or by any means, electronic, mechanical,
photocopying, recording or otherwise, without the prior
permission in writing of the publisher and the copyright
owners, or as expressly permitted by law, or under terms
agreed with the appropriate reprographics rights
organization. Enquiries concerning reproduction outside the
terms stated here should be sent to the publishers at the UK
address printed on this page.

The publisher makes no representation, express or implied,
with regard to the accuracy of the information contained in
this book and cannot accept any legal responsibility for any
errors or omissions that may be made.

A CIP catalogue record for this book is available from
the British Library.

ISBN: 978-1-85858-590-1

Printed and bound in Great Britain
by Hobbs the Printers Ltd.

Preface

When I was seven, I was sitting with my parents and brothers around the dinner table one evening and I was telling them about the history lesson I'd had earlier at school about Alfred the Great, the Saxon king. When I'd finished telling them about him, my father said "Did you know that Alfred the Great's surname was the same as ours - Pottinger - and we are all his descendants?" We all laughed and then my father said "If you don't believe me, ask your teacher tomorrow."

The next day, I went to school, stood up in class and said to my history teacher "Did you know that Alfred the Great's surname was Pottinger and our family are descended from him?" My teacher looked down at me and asked "Who told you that?" I stood very proudly and said "My dad." A smile came across his face and then he gave me a clip across my left ear, saying "That's for being cheeky." Then he gave me a clip across my right ear and said "And that's for having an idiot for a father!" The rest of the class laughed at my 'put down' and for weeks afterwards I was called King Alf.

Chapter One

I was born in Cheltenham maternity hospital on 3rd September 1943. I was the youngest of four boys, the eldest being John, then Gordon, Gerald and myself.

My dad was a simple man. He was one of fourteen children and was therefore used to 'going without'. He'd worked as a farm labourer for most of his adult life but one special gift he had was how he handled horses. He would talk to them in a gentle voice and could get a horse to do almost anything for him.

He didn't earn much in wages so it was left to my poor old mum to make ends meet. She had to feed and clothe four growing sons on very little money. To make up the deficit, she would grow vegetables and rear chickens (and sometimes pigs) which she would fatten up for us to eat.

The first place I can remember is a little village called Meysey Hampton which is about six miles from Cirencester. I can just remember living in a row of small cottages in what was called 'up the lane'. We moved from there to a bigger cottage on the village green. I liked living there because we had more room. It had three bedrooms. The bedroom doors opened outwards because when the beds were in the room, the door wouldn't open inwards. I shared a bed with my eldest brother John, and Gordon and Gerald shared the third bedroom. Our clothes hung on hooks on the wall because we had no room for wardrobes or chest of drawers.

There was no electricity or water in the house. We used paraffin lamps for light and our water was taken from the well on the village green. I remember that I liked to help my dad get the water from the well. We would take two buckets with us to fill and bring back home. At the well, there was a bucket with a rope attached and this, in turn, was attached to a handle. Dad would lower the bucket down the well and bring up some water. Then he would transfer the water from the bucket to our own two buckets that we'd brought with us. Dad carried the water using a 'yoke'. A yoke is a length of wood about five feet long with a length of chain with a hook on each end. Dad would put a bucket on each hook and then put the yoke across his shoulders so that when he stood up, his shoulders took the weight of the water.

We had a large garden at the back of the cottage where dad grew all kinds of vegetables. In one corner of the garden we had a chicken pen and coop which housed lots of chickens and a big red rooster. The rooster was nearly as tall as me and I was a bit afraid of him. I used to get a stick and poke him through the wire fencing. One day, I was helping my mum to collect the eggs, when the rooster ran across the pen and pecked me very hard on my leg which made me cry. My mum shooed him away saying "You must have done something to annoy him!" I never poked that rooster again.

We had a bench beside the front door of the cottage overlooking the village green. I remember sitting on the bench to watch people coming to and from the well for water. Sometimes it would be our neighbours and at other times a farmhand would bring his horse and cart so that he could 'water' the horse. I loved to run over to them and stroke these gentle animals and, if I was lucky, I would be allowed to sit on the horse's back while they drank the water.

One day while I was watching two farm hands watering their horses, I saw a tractor chugging past the village green, pulling two trailers full of hay. Tractors were a new thing in those days, so I was really excited to watch it going past. The two farmhands were looking at the tractor and one was saying to the other "They won't last! They'll never take the place of a good horse." I didn't really understand what they were saying as I was only three years old at the time.

I was born at a time of great change. It was wonderful to see a car or bus coming through the village but most of the farm work was still done by horses.

When I was four years old I started at the village school. I thought it was a great adventure. My three older brothers were all there and I soon made friends with the other children. The school had two classrooms. They were split into two age groups: younger children (up to seven years old) and older children (from seven to eleven).

I can't remember if I learnt much at my first school but I do remember an instance when I was in trouble with a teacher. On top of the school roof was a bell which the older boys would try to hit with stones to make it ring. I decided that it looked fun, so started throwing stones too but my aim was not as good as the bigger boys and they fell well short. Just at the moment I had thrown a stone, one of the teachers (Miss Jones) walked out of the door beneath the bell and was hit on the arm by my stone. She was not amused and looked around for the culprit - me! By then, the older boys had run off but I was rooted to the spot with a look of horror on my face. "I will see you tomorrow morning" she said.

I dreaded tomorrow morning at school and knew it was possible that I would get caned. I tried to think of a way out of my predicament. The next morning came and I told my mum that I wasn't feeling well, I couldn't possibly go to school. She knew that I was 'swinging the lead' and told me I would feel better when I got to school. I shuffled off, dreading the moment when I would face Miss Jones.

On the way there, I saw a group of girls making daisy chains. I watched fascinated for a while as they split the stems of the little white flower and then joined them together to make a chain. They would then put the 'chain' around their neck. I asked one of the girls to make one for me which she was happy to do. Then I put it up my jumper, out of sight and set off for school.

The school bell rang promptly at nine o'clock as I went into the playground. I lined up with the other children and then went into the classroom and sat at my desk. Miss Jones told us to sit down and be quiet.

She opened the register and started to call out our names, to which we answered "Yes Miss". I was hoping she had forgotten yesterday's incident but as she came to my name she said loudly "Richard Pottinger - come to the front of the class!" I felt my face go red as I got up from my seat and walked with wobbly legs to where the teacher sat at her desk at the front of the class. The other children watched and waited to see what I had done wrong.

I stood in front of her desk and lifted my head to look at her. She looked ten feet tall and was glaring down at me. I could feel my bottom lip quivering. After what seemed an age, Miss Jones said "Yesterday... what have you to say for yourself?" I didn't know what to say or do, so I reached under my jumper and found the daisy chain and held it up to Miss Jones. She glared at it, then at me. I could see her face soften and then a little smile played at the side of her mouth. "Are you sorry for throwing stones?" she said. I answered meekly "Yes". In a soft voice she told me to go back to my desk. What a relief!

I remember my fifth birthday. My mum had agreed to my plea for a birthday party. I was so excited that I rushed off to school and invited everyone I met to my party. I think I must have got carried away because the teacher came around to see my mum to explain that I had invited the whole school. My mum at first was shocked as there were about thirty-four children in the school and she couldn't afford to feed them all. The teacher said that all the children were excited about the party and looking forward to coming. She saw the look on my mum's face and told her that something would be sorted out. There were other children in the school with birthdays around this time, so it was arranged that the other mums would help out with the food and arrange a party on the village green for all the school children that I'd invited.

It was 1948 and some food was still on ration but all the families contributed something to the party. The day was wonderful. The parents put up the tables and chairs and helped to lay the tables with all sorts of food including cakes and drinks. We were fussed over by the mums, dads and teachers and after we had eaten that lovely party food we all played games. The sun shone brightly that day, the day that thirty-four children aged between four and eleven sat down to a lovely party and played games on the green. The war had finished three years before and one lady at the party said "That party was just what we all needed to cheer us up!" I will never forget my fifth birthday.

Chapter Two

When I was about six years old, my dad came home one day and spoke two words which I was to hear many times over the next few years, "We're shiftin'!" Those words meant we were moving house because my dad had lost his job on the farm and, as the house was tied to the job (i.e. a tied cottage), it meant we would have to move out so that the replacement farm labourer could move in.

I didn't know why my dad lost his job so often because you just couldn't ask questions like that in those days. He seemed to get on with everyone but my mum said that my dad would get angry with anyone being cruel to horses, so I think that may have been the reason he had to leave his job.

My mum was unhappy about moving out because she loved our cottage on the green but she had no say in the matter. It had been decided for her. My dad had got a job on another farm about four miles away in a little hamlet called Honeycomb Leaze. I didn't want to move out either and nor did my brothers because we would have to leave behind our village friends. Four miles in those days was a long way from friends and the people we'd got to know. It meant that we would also have to change schools.

My dad was going to work on a farm where they still used horses to do the farm work. The farmer lent my dad a horse and cart to carry our possessions. It took two trips to move everything to our new cottage.

Our new home was very much the same as the old one. It had no electricity but it did have running water. This was provided by a large water tank on a high wooden platform which was placed over a well. The water was pumped up from the well into the tank and then a pipe was attached to the tank which ran across a field and up to the cottage.

The cooking was done on a 'range'. This was made of iron with three compartments. The middle compartment contained the fire with a water tank on one side and a cooking oven on the other. The top was used as a 'hot plate'. Above the range there was a brass rail for hanging your cooking pots and pans. When the fire in the range was lit, it warmed the room. Lovely in winter but stiflingly hot in summer.

The nearest shop was five miles away in a larger village called Poulton where there was a shop and bakery. My dad acquired a bike so that my elder brothers could take it in turns to cycle to Poulton to buy any groceries we needed. Most things were still on ration at this time but we always had plenty of meat and vegetables. The meat was often supplied by the farmer, who would shoot a rabbit, hare, pigeon or pheasant and then share them with his neighbours.

I remember my time at Honeycomb Leaze with affection. My dad would often take me with him when working on the farm. I loved to watch him working with the farm horses. He would speak very gently to them and they would respond to his commands. He would always say that if you gained their confidence, they would do anything for you.

His favourite was a big shire horse which he called Old Bon. These were the giants among horses with enormous feet but I never felt afraid when standing next to them. Sometimes dad would lift me up and put me on Old Bon's back. The horse would whinny as if to tell me that he was enjoying it too.

I was out in the field one day, helping to cut kale (a kind of small green cabbage on a tall stem used for food to feed the cattle and sheep). My dad cut it with a large knife and I would help him to put the kale onto the cart which was pulled by Old Bon.

I heard a noise above us and stood watching a small plane flying around. My dad said it was a 'Harvard' trainer plane. I was fascinated watching the little plane going up and down and doing turns. Suddenly, it's engine started to splutter and then stop. It turned over and started to dive towards the ground. It crashed with an almighty 'bang', the loudest sound I'd ever heard. Old Bon, who was usually so calm, suddenly burst into life and bolted across the field, the cart bumping along behind him. Unfortunately, at the end of field was a deep ditch. Old Bon didn't see it until the last minute but he managed to jump the ditch, although the cart didn't quite make it and smashed into the side of the ditch and broke into hundreds of pieces. Old Bon still kept going though, pulling the remains of the cart behind him. Dad ran after him and eventually caught him up and calmed him down. Then he led the horse back to the farm, quietly reassuring Old Bon that everything was okay.

After an hour or so, an ambulance and fire engine appeared in the field where the plane had crashed but dad wouldn't let me anywhere near them. Looking back, he was probably protecting me from what I might see at the crash site.

A week later dad came home looking very upset and told us that Old Bon had injured himself when he had bolted across the field. When I learnt that he had been put in a small paddock next to the farmhouse, I decided to go to see him to check that he was alright. When I got there, I could see that he was looking stressed, so I went over to him and looked up at this giant of a horse, who looked down at me and then lowered his great head so that he looked straight into my face. Then he gave a quiet kind of a whinny as if to say "I'm okay. Don't worry!" I think he was glad to see me. He'd hurt his front left leg when he'd jumped the ditch and was having difficulty standing on it.

For the next two days, dad gave him hay and water and fussed over him, giving him treats such as carrots and apples. On the second day, the farmer told us that he had sent for the vet to check out Old Bon. I asked dad if the vet would make him better but I was told we would have to wait and see.

The next day I went off to school. I told my friends about the horse and that the vet was coming to the farm to make him better. When I got home I ran to the paddock to see Old Bon but he wasn't there. The paddock was empty. I wasn't too worried though. I thought perhaps the vet had made him better and that he was working in the fields. I wandered off to search for him but I couldn't find him anywhere. I ran from field to field in a wild panic. Where was he? I found my dad sitting on a bale of straw looking very sad. When I asked him about Old Bon he said "Come and sit down. I've something to tell you."

We sat down on the bale of straw and dad took my hands in his while he told me how the vet couldn't save Old Bon and the poor old horse had to be put down. My heart sank and I shook my head refusing to believe it. "We could have looked after him" I told my dad but he told me that the horse had broken his leg and was in great pain. It was a kindness to put him out of his misery.

I was heartbroken and burst into tears, tearing myself away from my dad's grasp and ran home. Mum was by the door when I got there and she picked me up and hugged me tight. She told me that I must be brave and that Old Bon had gone to a lovely place in the sky.

I will always remember that wonderful old horse.

Living in the countryside, you had to get used to animals that died and got taken away. Sheep, cattle and pigs were eventually all taken away to market to be sold and pheasants, pigeons and rooks were regularly shot. It was also a regular thing to see my dad kill a chicken for the pot.

The summer after Old Bon died, the farmer bought a new tractor. He said that you had to 'move with the times'. The day of the working farm horse was fading fast. I'd witnessed the end of an era.

Summer on the farm was always a joy, especially when it was harvest time. The harvest consisted of mainly wheat and barley. A tractor pulled what we call a 'binder' which would cut the corn and send it up onto a conveyor belt. Then it was 'bunched' together and tied with string to form a sheaf. This would then be thrown out of the binder and onto the ground. The sheaves would then be picked up by hand and stacked together, ready to be collected and taken to the farm. At the farm, the sheaves would be stacked into giant 'ricks' about thirty feet high. They would then be thatched with straw to keep them dry.

At harvest time, the farmers always helped each other to get the harvest in while the weather was fine. I loved this time of year. My brothers and I would join together with other children from neighbouring farms and help to stack the sheaves. There would always be lots of rabbits in the cornfield and, as the corn was cut, the rabbits would run out of their hiding place where we were waiting to chase them with a stick. If we were lucky, we would catch them but you had to be quick and anticipate where they would run.

I remember one day the gamekeeper turned up at the field and he told us not to chase the rabbits because he wanted to use his shotgun to shoot them. We were told to stay out of his way but one young lad called Pete Cook, forgetting that we had been told to stay well clear, decided to chase a rabbit he'd spotted in the corn. I heard a loud bang as the shotgun was fired but the gamekeeper missed the rabbit and hit my friend Pete. When the shotgun pellets hit him, he jumped screaming into the air.

The farmer driving the tractor jumped down and ran over to Pete, cursing at the gamekeeper for what he'd done to the lad. He told the gamekeeper to go quickly to the farmhouse to ask his wife for some towels. I'd never seen anyone shot before and was horrified at what I saw. The farmer was very calm and reassuring, telling me that it was not as bad as it looked and that the lad would be alright.

Pete was still screaming when the farmer's wife arrived with the towels but she calmed him down by talking softly to him and quickly wrapped him up with the towels and carried him to the farmhouse. Later an ambulance arrived to take the lad to hospital where he stayed for a week. When he at last came home, he was fussed over and spoilt by his mum and sisters. They were obviously relieved that he had been relatively unscathed but we were all envious of the attention he was getting.

The shooting was the talk of the neighbourhood. Questions were asked as to how it had happened but eventually was recorded as an 'accidental discharge'.

Soon afterwards, another incident happened which made everyone forget all about the shooting. There was an airbase about four miles away just outside a town called Fairford. The airbase was used by the American Air Force. Big American planes would roar low over our houses, getting ready to land.

One night, I was awakened by a loud thunderous rumbling sound. I jumped out of bed and rushed to the window to see what was going on. I could see a red glow in the sky a distance away. I called my brothers to the window and asked them what it could be. My eldest brother said that it was probably an explosion at the airbase. A plane must have crashed on landing. We were told to go back to bed by our parents but we could hear alarm bells and could see bright lights coming from the base and we couldn't sleep.

In the morning, as soon as it was light, my brothers and I set off over the fields towards the airbase. It wasn't long before we found out what had caused the explosion the night before. An enormous transport plane had crashed just short of the landing strip and exploded. All the contents of the plane were scattered everywhere. There were police and MPs (military police) all over the field, trying to prevent the locals getting too close to the crash site. The plane had been carrying supplies to the airbase.

We could see that the boxes on the plane had been full of wonderful food that we hadn't seen for ages, if at all. There were tins of peaches, pears, tinned meat and fish and, best of all, sweets and chocolate bars. Most food was still on ration at this time, even though the war had finished five years earlier, so these goods were a luxury to us.

When we thought it was safe, my brothers and I sneaked back to the crash site and scooped up as much of the goodies as we could and set off across the fields back home but we then had to find somewhere to 'stash' them. One of us came up with the idea of putting them in the old shed at the top of the garden. My brothers decided to go back for more but I stayed on in the shed and tucked into a chocolate bar. Wow, did it taste good!

My brothers came back loaded down with more tins and chocolate which we pushed into a corner of the shed and covered with an old sheet. I wanted to tell my mum about our 'loot' but my brothers made me promise not to tell. Not at the moment anyway.

For the next few days, there was a lot of activity around the airbase. Dad told us that the police and MPs were looking for the missing cargo from the crashed plane and anyone found to be harbouring any of it would go to jail. I was really frightened and wanted to tell my mum about our hoard in the shed but my brothers told me to stay quiet and that things would 'blow over'.

Two days later I was playing at the farm when two policemen and two American military policemen drove into the yard in a jeep. They got out and walked over to the farmer and started to talk to him. I moved closer to hear what they were saying and heard the word 'contraband'. I didn't know anyone called Contraband. I thought I would go home and ask my mum if she knew anyone with that name.

When I got home, I saw my brothers John and Gordon lurking behind the garden shed. John called me over and asked what the MPs were doing at the farm. I told him they were looking for someone called Contraband. A look of horror came across their faces and they started to discuss moving the supplies from the shed to a safer place. It was then that we saw the two MPs walking up the garden path to our house. They looked like giants!

They knocked on the door and then my mum answered it and asked how she could help them. They told her that they were looking for supplies taken from the crashed plane. They went on to say that they had a warrant to search any premises suspected of harbouring the supplies. Mum invited them in with a smile and shut the door. My brothers looked at each other and then decided to quickly move the goods out of the shed but realised that the door to the shed faced the house and we could be seen.

After about ten minutes John looked at me and said, that as I was the youngest and most innocent-looking, I should go to the house and see what was happening inside. I shook my head and refused. I was scared of those two big men and thought they might start asking me a lot of questions. John was determined it should be me and started to push me towards the house, as he retreated to the safety of the shed. I crept towards the house, my heart pounding. I looked back at John and he was waving me on.

As I entered the house and shut the door, the MPs turned to look at me from the kitchen table where they were sat talking to my mum. I felt doomed. A smile broke out on the two MPs' faces. As I walked towards them, one of the men picked me up and sat me on his knee saying "Is this the little fella in the photo?" Mum had made them some tea and was showing them some family photos and, in turn, the two men were showing mum some photos of their families back home in America.

When they had chatted and laughed for a while, the two men said they had to go and made their way towards the door. Mum followed them and asked if they wanted to look around the rest of the house before they left but one of them said "No thank you ma'am, that won't be necessary."

They left the house and were walking down the path when, to our horror, mum called out to them that we had a garden shed and they might want to look inside. From the door I looked across at my brothers who were lurking behind the shed and I held my breath. "No, that's fine ma'am. We don't need to look but thank you for the tea" they said, and continued on their way.

When our mum and dad found out what was in the garden shed, they were not too pleased. John and Gordon had a good telling off for corrupting Gerald and myself in helping them to break the law. Over the following weeks we all enjoyed the tins of peaches and pears and especially the chocolate bars which tasted like nothing we'd had before. We broke them into small pieces to make them last longer.

I was very happy living at Honeycomb Leaze. There were several other farms scattered around the area and we had friends living on most of them.

What I remember most about those days was the freedom to roam around the countryside. One of our pastimes was collecting birds' eggs. Most of us had a prized collection. I kept mine in a cardboard box about eighteen inches square. In the box I had a layer of fine sawdust and would push the eggs into the sawdust to hold the eggs firm. I had about thirty to forty different eggs in my collection. Most birds laid around four eggs but we would only take one egg from each nest, then the bird would lay another one to take its place.

There were more birds around in those days and you learnt how to find their nest. They would be found in hedgerows, walls or barns, as well as in the trees or on the ground. My elder brothers taught me how to find the birds which nested on the ground. The parent birds would never fly straight to the nest as they didn't want predators to locate it, so they would land a few yards away, look around to check that it was safe, and then walk to the nest which would be hidden by foliage on the ground.

The most prized eggs belonged to swans and rooks because you had to be very brave to take them. Swans were very protective of their eggs. You had to wait until both swans were away from the nest in search of food and then creep up to the nest without the adult swans seeing you and steal an egg. If they saw you, they would attack quite viciously.

Rooks and crows build their nest on the highest branches of the trees. As I was the smallest and lightest of my brothers, it was my job to climb the trees to take the eggs from the nest. The branches at the top were quite thin and would sway in the breeze and when I got close to the nest the branch would bend because of my weight on it, but all the same I had to slowly edge my way along the branch to the nest, all the time being egged on by my brothers on the ground.

When I reached for the eggs, I put them one by one into a bag that I had around my neck, being very careful not to break any of them before I reached the ground. John would make me get several of these 'hard to get' eggs and would then sell them for sixpence each to the boys at school who were afraid to climb to the top of the trees.

It was a long way to school from our home in Honeycomb Leaze. My eldest brother John had to go to the 'big' school (secondary modern) in Fairford about five miles away. He was the lucky one. Being the eldest, he had the use of the family bike but Gordon, Gerald and I had to walk about a mile from the farm until we reached the crossroads, where we would meet up with three other children from nearby farms to wait for a taxi that had been arranged for us to be taken to school at Poulton about four miles away.

I had never been in a car before and I loved it. Gerald and I attended Poulton Village School but Gordon had won a place at Cirencester Grammar School. To get to the grammar school, Gordon had to take a bus from Poulton to Cirencester about five miles away.

Chapter Three

Things changed very quickly. One day dad came into the house and said those dreaded words "We're shiftin'!" I watched my mum's shoulders drop as she said "Not again. What's happened now?" He told her that he'd had an argument with the farmer who had then sacked him. The house we lived in was a 'tied cottage', therefore it belonged to the farm. This meant that we would have to move out. My mum, looking downhearted asked him what would happen to us but dad's reply was always "Don't worry, summat'll turn up!"

I felt so sorry for my mum. She had worked hard to make this little house into a home. I could see the tears welling up in her eyes as she looked out of the window to where she could see the vegetables starting to grow but not ready to be picked yet.

The next few days felt very strange. My brothers and I went off to school as usual and after a while we thought maybe we would not be moving after all.

Those thoughts were dashed one day when we came home from school to find the farmer showing some tenants around the house. I heard my mum telling the farmer that we would be moving as soon as my dad could find a new job and somewhere else to live. The farmer gave us a week to move out or we would be forcibly removed. Mum was very upset when dad came home and they argued because dad still had no job lined up or anywhere else to live. As usual he said "Don't worry. Summat'll turn up!"

Well something did turn up because a few days later dad came home with a smile on his face with the good news that he had another job on a farm near Poulton. We would be moving into a bungalow in the village. I didn't know what a bungalow was, so I asked Gerald who told me that it was a house that had no bedrooms upstairs.

My dad borrowed an old lorry to carry our possessions to the bungalow. We all had to help to fill the boxes and load the lorry. Dad lit a bonfire in the garden to burn anything that we couldn't take with us or we didn't need. I got very upset when I realised that dad had thrown my bird egg collection on the fire but he told me not to worry, I could collect some more later.

After all our possessions were packed onto the lorry, it was time to leave. I was very upset leaving Honeycomb Leaze. I'd grown very fond of the old cottage and my secret little dens around the farm. My mum put her arms around me and told me I would like it a lot better when we got to Poulton and that I must look on the move as a great new adventure.

Mum was right. I enjoyed the ride with my brothers on the back of the lorry, sat among the household furniture.

Our new home in Poulton was a bungalow. All the rooms were on the ground floor. I'd never seen this before and then remembered Gerald telling me it was a house with no bedrooms upstairs but I thought that meant it had no bedrooms at all. I was relieved to find it had three bedrooms and an inside toilet. There was also a kitchen with running water and best of all, electric light in every room. It was lovely.

Mum was really excited when she went into the kitchen and saw a modern wood-burning Aga cooker. We couldn't believe the space we had. In the old place, all four brothers had to share one bedroom. Now there would be only two in each bedroom.

The bungalow had a large garden and a new chicken pen which dad had put up. Dad and John enjoyed marking out the vegetable patch.

We soon settled into our new home but it did take a while to get used to sleeping downstairs.

My dad was pleased to have moved back to Poulton, the village where he was born as one of fourteen children. His parents (my grandparents) and six of his brothers and a sister still lived in the village.

My brother Gerald and I were pleased that the village school was only half a mile away and Gordon didn't have to walk far to get the bus to the grammar school in Cirencester. It was about this time that my eldest brother John left school and got a job as an apprentice carpenter.

The next two years were a joy to me and my family. My gran and grandad lived just down the road. I loved to visit them because they always made a fuss of me, being the youngest, and gave me homemade cake.

I remember my grandparents had a new toilet built onto the side of the house. It was a chemical toilet which would be emptied every two weeks by the local council. My gran was told that the chemicals could be explosive, so smoking was not allowed in there. Grandad wasn't happy about that. He enjoyed smoking his pipe and reading his newspaper while sitting on the toilet. It was the highlight of his day! Gran would not relent, so grandad had to use the old earth closet at the top of the garden (we called it 'the night fighter').

I don't think grandad really minded. Having fourteen children, it was the only place he could get some peace and quiet.

The village had a post office, grocery store, butcher's shop and bakery. The smell of baking bread was wonderful. Every Tuesday Mr. Ash, the baker, would make trays of sticky lardy cake. After he'd tipped the lardy cake out of the trays, there would be a thick layer of sticky crust left around the edge of the tray and he would let us young lads scrape the crust off the sides and eat it. It smelt and tasted lovely.

We were all really happy living in Poulton. We had aunts, uncles and several cousins all living within walking distance. My mum was very happy with her new Aga cooker. There were three hot plates on the top and two ovens below.

My dad soon had the chicken pen stocked with lots of chickens, which before long were laying lots of lovely fresh eggs.

While living at Poulton, I saw lots of changes going on around me. The farm horses were disappearing and tractors were taking their place. Cars were starting to appear. One of our hobbies was sitting on the side of the road taking car registration numbers. Some days we might see as many as ten cars!

I enjoyed going to school in the village. My brother Gerald and several cousins went to the school. The teachers made learning fun. They would take us out for walks in the countryside and would teach us about nature.

There were sad times too. The school playground had got lots of pot holes and when it rained, it could get really muddy. Someone decided it was a good idea to cover the playground with gravel. This wasn't a good idea. Young boys like to throw stones. We also loved to put glass bottles and jars on the top of a wall and see who could break the most with the stones we picked up.

At the one end of the playground was a tin shed with no roof on it which served as the pupils' toilets. We would wait until someone used the toilets and then start throwing stones at it. When they landed on the tin it sounded like firing a machine gun. This would scare the kids inside and they would come running out. We thought this was very funny until one day a young lad called Peter came running out because he was so frightened and a stray stone struck his eye. He fell to the ground screaming with pain.

One of the teachers came out to see what all the noise was about and was really shocked to see what had happened to Peter. It was such a serious injury that he was taken to hospital and eventually lost the sight in that eye.

There were a lot of recriminations about what had happened. All the boys were blaming each other. The headmaster gathered all the boys together who had been in the playground at the time and told us that we were all guilty and should be ashamed of ourselves. I think we were remorseful and very sorry for what we'd done but poor Peter had still lost the sight in his eye.

Chapter Four

My Uncle Bert was a strange man. He had a hunchback. I asked him one day why he had a big hump on his back and he told me that it was because he was born back to front!

Uncle Bert loved his garden and he would let me help him to sow seeds and plants but he had a problem with the next door neighbour's cat that was digging holes in his garden. He told me that with my help he could persuade the cat not to dig holes.

We found a spot in the garden where the soil was soft and Uncle Bert instructed me to dig a hole about a foot deep. On the edge of the hole, Uncle Bert put some titbits of food, then we walked back towards the house and I sat on a bench while Uncle Bert went into the house and came out again holding a shotgun. He laid it across his lap and said we were to sit quietly and wait.

We must have been sat quietly for about half an hour when the cat appeared in the garden. It looked around and slowly made its way across the garden to where I had dug the hole and started to eat the food we had left there. Uncle Bert raised the shotgun to his shoulder and made to fire it. I tugged on his sleeve and pleaded with him not to shoot the cat and telling him that it was cruel but he didn't take his eyes off the cat as he said "I know what I'm doing". The gun went off with a loud bang.

The cat shot up into the air with fright and landed with its tail bolt upright, then ran for its life out of the garden, the way it had come. Uncle Bert turned to me and said "If you don't want a cat coming unwanted into your garden, you have to give it a good fright."

I asked him why I had dug the hole in the garden and Uncle Bert looked down at me and, tapping the side of his nose with his finger, he replied "The cat knows!" Just like I said before - my Uncle Bert was a strange man.

I was very happy living in Poulton. There was always something to do. In summer, we would go out in the morning and not come back until teatime. Mum would say "They'll come home when they're hungry".

There were several farms scattered around the village. After school, we would call at the farm and talk to the farmhands. They would give us little jobs to do. It taught us, at an early age, how to do things properly and safely. I used to watch the cows being milked in the farm's dairy. After the milk had been cooled, it would be poured into the milk churns and placed on a platform by the gate, ready to be picked up by a lorry and then taken to the main dairy in Cirencester. Anyone who worked on the farm would have free milk.

A job I really loved was helping the ferret man. A ferret man's job was to keep the rabbit numbers down. Rabbits were a pest. They would eat almost anything and ruin the crops. Rabbits lived underground in warrens which were made up of interlocking tunnels with several exits. Rabbits were very shy animals and could hear you coming before you caught sight of them and would run and hide in the warren.

The ferret man would put nets over all the exit holes except one. This one was where the ferret would enter the warren. A ferret looks a bit like a stoat or weasel but bigger and is really vicious. You had to handle them very carefully so that you didn't get bitten. The ferret man would tie a length of string to the ferret, so that he could retrieve it when it had done its work. Then he would put the ferret into the hole and wait.

If everything went to plan, the frightened rabbits would run out of the warren and into the nets. It was my job to catch the rabbit before it could escape from the net and pass it to the ferret man who would strike it over the head with a wooden club.

The rabbits were sold to the people in the village for a shilling each but I was paid for my help in rabbits. Usually one or two for free to take home to my family. My mum would skin and dress them, ready for the pot. Rabbit stew mixed with potatoes and carrots tasted wonderful.

In the centre of the village was a big house. We thought the people who lived there were very posh. They had a big car and talked 'funny'. The house had a five-foot wall dividing their garden from the public footpath. Behind the wall was a noisy green parrot in a cage. People would talk to the parrot when they walked past. Over time the parrot learnt some words like "Hello" or "Pretty Boy". We thought it was very funny when someone taught him to say swear words. There was uproar when he came out with "Knickers off!"

The village had a good cricket pitch and pavilion. In summer on Sunday afternoons, cricket matches would be played. A good crowd would turn out to watch the match. My two elder brothers sometimes played for the team. Gordon was making quite a name for himself at cricket.

Scouts from more successful sides came to see him play and he ended up playing for Cirencester.

When the day was clear and warm, the girls and ladies would lay tables for tea, laden with sandwiches and cakes for the players. The younger children would try to steal the cakes when the ladies weren't looking.

There was a stream that flowed past the village and at one point, the stream broadened out into a pool and, on hot summer days, we would swim and have water fights. My brothers used to call the pool Charlem Docks.

A day I will never forget was the first time I went to the seaside. A coach had been laid on to take people from Poulton to Weston super Mare. Our mum paid for herself, Gordon, Gerald and me to go. When the day arrived, our family and friends set off for Weston. We were all very excited because most of us had never seen the sea.

It was a long journey and the old coach we were travelling in struggled to get up some of the hills on the way there. When it made it to the top, we would all cheer. We also cheered when we arrived at Weston and had our first glimpse of the sea.

The coach drew up on the seafront and everyone got off. I was so excited to see such a large expanse of water that just seemed to go on and on for as far as I could see. Gordon, Gerald and their mates wanted to go to the beach. Mum and her friends wanted to go around the shops. Mum asked me what I wanted to do and I said I wanted to go to the shops with her but as we started to walk along the road I changed my mind and thought I would have more fun with my brothers on the beach. "If that's what you want to do" my mum said "you had better run and catch them up."

I ran back to the beach but I couldn't find them. I searched everywhere but still couldn't see them. I began to panic. I couldn't see anyone I knew - my brothers or my mum. I ran up and down the road calling for my mum but I couldn't find her. I suddenly felt terrified and all alone, sitting on the pavement and sobbing noisily. A kind lady came over to me and asked why I was crying. Between sobs, I told her that I was lost. She said that she would find a policeman who would help me to find my mum.

When he arrived, he asked me my name and told me not to worry - he would find her. He started shouting in a loud voice "Has anyone lost a child!" The chant was echoed down the beach by different people to reach everyone's ears but still no sign of anyone coming to claim me. The policeman turned to me and said "Looks like you've been abandoned young man! We'll have to walk to the police station and wait there. We'll get you a cup of tea if you like?"

At the police station, the sergeant looked me up and down and said "Looks like a bank robber to me!" But that just made me sob even more, crying "I'm not, I'm not. I've lost my mum". The policeman that brought me in explained that he had tried to locate my mum by calling out down the length of the beach but had no response, so he would have to go out into the town to see if he could find her.

I stayed in the station all day. The policemen did their best to cheer me up and keep me occupied but I just wanted my mum. It was about 6 pm before the sergeant received a phone call from a very anxious mother looking for her son. When she eventually arrived, I ran to her and she picked me up and hugged me. The kindly sergeant asked her why she hadn't heard the call down the beach about a lost boy but mum said she thought I was with my brother Gordon until she saw Gordon who told her I wasn't with him either.

The sergeant accepted my mum's explanation and wished us well as we left, ruffling my hair and telling me to keep hold of my mum's hand next time.

The coach was waiting to take us home and as we boarded a great cheer went up. They had all been worried too and were glad to see the family reunited. On the way home, everyone was talking about the lovely day they'd had but I felt even more miserable. I'd spent the whole day in jail!

Chapter Five

It was lovely to be part of a large extended family here in Poulton and we felt part of the village community but this was about to change yet again.

It was 1951. I was eight years old, and one evening when we were sat around the kitchen table, Mum was serving us some tea when dad walked into the kitchen and stood in front of us, cigarette dangling from his mouth. It was then he uttered the dreaded words "We're shiftin'!" Mum dropped the plate she was carrying and asked him why we were moving. "I suppose you've got the sack again!" John and Gordon looked worried. They were both working now and another move could mean a loss of their jobs and, for Gerald and I, a move to yet another school. Mum continued "This is the best home we've ever had. Why have you got to spoil it by moving us on? What will happen to us and where will we go?" My dad's reply was something I'd heard many times before "Oh, summat'll turn up!"

My dad was not a bad man. He worked very hard and would give anyone his last penny. I think he was just a weak man who would say the wrong thing at the wrong time to the wrong people.

The next week or so was terrible. We all loved living in Poulton. Gerald and I loved the village school. We all hoped dad would get his job back and that we wouldn't have to move after all but this didn't happen, and we were faced with eviction because it was a tied cottage which went with the job. I was really sad to be leaving and that I wouldn't be part of village life anymore.

At school, we had been rehearsing for the Christmas Panto and I had been given a good part. It really hurt to be told by my teacher that I was to be taken out of the panto because I might not be here at Christmas. That night I was in tears as I told my mum about losing my part in the panto saying "It's not fair". She replied "Life's not fair!" and you can't argue with that.

My dad seemed to have a knack for finding new jobs. He had a new job as a gamekeeper and the house came with the job. The job was in a hamlet called Furzen Leaze near Cirencester.

Every time we moved my mum would bear the brunt of it. She was the one doing all the worrying. How to pay the outstanding bills to the baker and grocer. She had to pack our belongings into boxes. Some things we could take but others had to be left behind.

Chapter Six

The moving day arrived. My dad had arranged for a removals lorry to take us to our new home. We were all expected to help to load the lorry. All went well until dad tried to load the chickens. The driver was having none of it and told dad he would have to get a neighbour to take them off him. When we were ready to go, our nan and aunt came to see us off.

My brothers John and Gordon wouldn't be travelling with us. They couldn't get the time off work, so the plan was to ride their bikes to our new house after they'd finished work.

On the way out of the village, I looked out of the back of the lorry and saw people I knew going about their daily business and felt sad that I would no longer be part of their life.

It took about an hour to get to our new home. We wound our way along country lanes and then eventually turned off onto a farm track, arriving after half a mile to a farmhouse. The lorry stopped and we all got out to have a look around but we could only see the farmhouse and outbuildings. There were no other houses to be seen. The driver wondered if we had come to the right place but dad reassured him that we were where we were supposed to be. Mum asked dad if we were going to be living in the farmhouse. Dad said "No, but I'll show you where we are going to live."

He led us around the side of the farm buildings to a gate which opened up onto a grass field, and in turn led to another field. At the far end of the second field were two old cottages standing beside a large wood. There was no road or track which led to these cottages. I could see that mum was upset at being brought to such a desolate place. "Where have you brought us? I'm not living here!" she said. Dad said "Don't worry, you'll soon get used to the place."

We went back to the lorry and dad told the driver that our home was two fields away. The driver wouldn't take his lorry across the fields in case the lorry got stuck in the soft ground and he told us that we would have to unload our possessions onto the farmyard. We were horrified. How were we to get our things across the fields? At that moment the farmer appeared and asked if dad was the new gamekeeper. When dad had introduced himself and our family, the farmer suggested loading our things onto his tractor and trailer. What a relief! We wouldn't have to carry them ourselves.

The farmer asked the lorry driver to help us to unload at the cottage but the driver insisted he had only been asked to load and unload which is what he'd done. With a cheery wave to my dad and "Good luck mate! You'll need it" he drove away from the farmhouse and left us to sort ourselves out.

In an hour, we had loaded our things onto the trailer and we were off across the fields. The kindly farmer had taken pity on us, drove the tractor and helped with taking our things into the cottage at the other end. There was no room on the trailer for any of our family so we walked in silence behind the trailer.

When we arrived at the cottage, the farmer said "Welcome to your new home". The two cottages were attached to each other with another family living in the other cottage. Our possessions were unloaded and placed outside the door. The farmer got back on his tractor and left us to take our things inside. I looked over at mum who had started to cry. Dad tried to comfort her saying that it was only temporary and that anyway everything would look different when we'd got it all inside.

If we thought the outside looked bleak, we found the inside even less encouraging. The first room was the kitchen and scullery. On the one side of the room was the staircase leading to the bedrooms. On the far wall there was a fireplace with a wood-burning iron stove. To the left of the fireplace was a door leading to another room. On another wall were several shelves for storage.

There was a window that looked out into the wood and below the window was a crock sink. It was then that mum noticed that the sink had no taps or pipes attached to it. This meant that there was no running water. Looking around, we soon realised that there was no electricity either, so no electric lighting. Mum was crying and saying that this was the worst house she'd ever lived in. Dad tried to cheer her up by telling her it wasn't that bad but we knew that she was right.

Gerald and I decided to look at the bedrooms upstairs. There were three bedrooms but they were in a terrible state. Plaster was coming off the walls and the window frames were rotting. It looked a real mess and we were feeling so miserable and disappointed. We went back downstairs and found mum and dad in the back yard. Mum was having 'words' with dad about our predicament: no running water, no electricity and no toilet! Just at that moment our neighbour appeared in the doorway. He'd heard what mum had said and told us that there was a toilet. It was in the wood!

The man was scruffy-looking with grubby clothes and unshaven face. He told us his name was Ben Carter and that he lived next door with his wife, son, daughter and grandson. He asked us to follow him and he took us into the wood to see our toilet. It stood about fifteen yards from the door of the cottage and was really just a wooden shed, about 6 x 4 feet. Inside was a fixed bench with a round hole in it. Underneath had been dug a hole about three feet deep. This was our toilet!

Mum seemed to get her resolve back and began to take stock of how things were going to work out. She said that we were here and that we would have to make the most of it. She told me to go with Gerald to get some firewood so that she could light the wood-burning stove in the kitchen.

While we got the inside habitable, Mr. Carter helped dad to bring our possessions into the house. By the time all our things were inside, mum had got the fire going, boiled the kettle and made us all some tea. The water for the kettle had to be brought from the water butt. This was attached to the drainpipe from the guttering to collect the rainwater from the roof.

While we were drinking our tea, Mr. Carter told us that we could get fresh water from the farm because there was an outside tap attached to the water supply. The only problem was carrying it over two fields to get it home. He also said that a baker delivered fresh bread twice a week to the farm and that we could arrange for our order to be delivered there. Otherwise, it meant buying essentials from the local shop at Siddington which was two miles away. We would also need to buy paraffin from this shop so that we could light the Tilly Lamps for our lighting as the house had no electricity.

We had two Tilly Lamps which mum and dad had kept from the days when we needed them at Honeycomb Leaze. Dad drew a map of the area to show us the location of Siddington and then asked Gerald and I to go to the shop to buy paraffin and candles and gave us a container for the paraffin. We were both afraid to go in case we got lost on the way there but dad would have none of it and told us the quicker we set off in the light the better, or we would be coming back in the dark.

We set off across the fields to the farm, down the farm track and under a railway bridge. Then kept going for another half a mile until we reached a narrow road. We turned left and walked for nearly a mile before we reached the main road which led to Siddington.

We saw the village shop and walked in. The lady behind the counter looked at us kindly and asked us what we wanted. We told her that we needed paraffin and candles and she asked us how much money we had. When we told her two shillings, she told us we could have half a gallon of paraffin and two candles. We gave her the container and while she was filling it up, she asked us who we were and where we lived. We told her our names and about the cottage by the wood, next to the farm at Furzen Leaze. "Oh dear" she said "Be careful. The family next door to you are a bit mad." Gerald said we had met Mr. Carter from next door and he had helped us to move in. He seemed alright. With a smile she said "Wait until you meet the rest of the family!"

Gerald and I picked up the paraffin and candles, left the shop and started off on the long walk back home. When we got to the main road, we sat down on the grass verge to rest for a while. We noticed two people coming towards us on bicycles. We jumped up excitedly when we realised it was our brothers John and Gordon. After a day's work, they had met up in Cirencester and all they had was a note on a piece of paper that dad had given them with just the name of the farm on it. I think they were relieved to see us there so that we could show them the way to the cottage.

Gerald and I jumped up onto the handlebars and we all set off for home. When we got to the farm, our brothers were confused as to where our cottage could be. We pointed to distant buildings across the two fields and told them that it was over there. More shocks were in store for them when they saw the state of the cottage. It seemed amazing that in twenty-four hours we could go from living in a lovely bungalow with electric light and running water to this rundown cottage with no electricity, no running water and a dirt toilet in the wood.

We had to make the best of it. What else could we do? Mum took control as usual and gave everyone jobs to do. John and Gordon helped dad to get the beds made up and Gerald had to take some containers to the farm to collect some fresh water. I had to help mum in the kitchen and set about peeling some potatoes. We all had to get used to our new environment.

John and Gordon would ride their bikes into Cirencester to work. John was an apprentice carpenter and Gordon worked for the Corona (fizzy pop) company. Dad was working for the Earl Bathurst Estate as a gamekeeper. Gerald and I were given the job of fetching and carrying for mum.

We soon got to know our neighbours and, just as the lady at the shop had told us, they were a bit mad. Mr. Carter seemed friendly enough. He would come to talk to us when we were outside but we seldom saw Mrs. Carter or their daughter Ruth. Sometimes their son Terry, who was about twenty years old, would come over to talk to us but he was unwell a lot of the time, as he was prone to having fits. Their daughter had a little boy about two years old whose name was Sam. They had a collie dog called Barney who I took to straight away and loved to play with him.

Very often Mr. Carter would disappear for a few days and come back home roaring drunk. When he walked in the house all hell would break loose! There was a lot of shouting and swearing which got louder and louder. Sometimes Terry and the dog would sneak out of the house and hide in the wood.

Dad's new job as a gamekeeper gave us a good supply of pheasants, rabbits and pigeons, which would be dressed and made ready for the pot. Sometimes he would take me with him. He would tell me to go into the wood and then shout and clap my hands. This would frighten the birds and make them fly up into the air so that dad could shoot them. If he shot a pheasant, we would have it for the pot but if it was a magpie or jay, he would hang them on a fence. I didn't understand why we could eat pheasants but not magpies or jays. Dad said that a gamekeeper's job was to rear pheasants and partridges for the rich people to shoot.

All the woods and plantations were planted by the rich land owners so that the birds could live there and lay their eggs but magpies and jays were scavengers and they would eat the eggs of other birds. He explained that by hanging the dead magpies and jays on the fence, it was a warning to others of their kind not to eat other birds' eggs.

He went on to say that another reason for hanging the birds on a fence was to give food to the foxes. If we gave them magpies to eat, they would leave our chickens alone.

He also said that it was the gamekeeper's job to make sure that the people who attended the hunt had a good day out. When foxes are being chased by the foxhounds, they will run and hide in holes or drains. Therefore, the night before a hunt, dad would block up all the holes and drains in the area so that the fox had to stay above ground. This made the chase more enjoyable for the people on horseback. Somehow this didn't seem fair to me. It didn't give the fox a chance to escape.

A couple of days after our move, mum said that Gerald and I would have to be enrolled at the local school in Siddington. She cleaned us up and then we set off for the school two miles away. Siddington School was the usual kind of village school at the time. Two classes: one for the older children and one for the little ones. School had already started when we got there. Mum looked through one of the classroom windows and caught the eye of the teacher. He came to the window and she asked if we could be enrolled at the school.

We went inside and waited for him to take us into his office. His name was Mr. Stevens and he was the headmaster of the school. While Gerald and I sat nervously looking around us, mum gave him all the particulars he needed. Then he looked at Gerald and I and we could tell that he wasn't very impressed with what he saw. When mum told him where we lived he said "I thought those places had been condemned." Mum said "They should be!" We were then left at the school for the rest of the day. Mum giving us a cheery wave and telling us to do our best and be good.

Gerald and I were introduced to our class by Mr. Stevens. I went into the class for the little ones and Gerald was taken to the other class for the older children. My teacher was Miss Knight. She looked me up and down and then told me to stand in front of the class and tell the other children my name and where I lived. I was very shy and embarrassed, standing there facing all those children. When

I told them about the cottage by the wood with no running water or electricity, they looked horrified. It didn't make me feel any better when I looked into their faces.

I hated starting new schools. It meant trying to fit in and I never liked it or got used to it. The other children would stare at you with a natural curiosity and it wasn't long before one of the girls sidled up to me and said "I've heard about your neighbours The Carters. I've heard that they eat babies!"

I wanted to know more but the lesson had started and Miss Knight told everyone to be quiet. For the rest of the day, I tried to settle into school life but the children were not friendly like they had been at my school in Poulton.

On the way home I told Gerald what the girl had said about the Carters. I was worried that they might eat little Sam.

We all found it hard living at Furzen Leaze. We had to adapt to our new life. Whenever we went to the farm, we would have to take a water container and fill it up before we came back. When John and Gordon rode their bikes into Cirencester, mum would give them a list of things we needed to buy from the shop. Sometimes Gerald and I would have to go to the shop in Siddington on our way back home from school. We felt really tired by the time we had finished at school, done the shopping mum needed and then walked two miles home.

My brother Gerald and I didn't like Siddington School. We hated the two-mile walk to get there and if we were late, we would be punished by having a 12-inch ruler whacked across the back of our legs. My teacher, Miss Knight, owned a little car which she drove to school every day. She would pass us on the road but would never stop to give us a lift to school. She would just glare at us as she drove past.

I remember one day when it was raining really hard and we were getting soaking wet, she drove past and, as she did so, she looked at her watch and smiled. She knew we were going to be late - and we were! When Gerald and I arrived at school, Miss Knight was waiting for us by the main door with a ruler in her hand. All she said was "You're late" and smacked us both across the back of our legs. I don't think I had ever felt as miserable as I did that day.

My feet were sore from walking and my legs were stinging from my punishment. All this walking to school soon wore a hole in the sole of my shoes. Mum had to cut out strips of cardboard to fit into my shoes to make them last a bit longer. This sounds a good idea except that when it rained, the cardboard turned to mush and made my feet wet and sore.

However, it wasn't all 'doom and gloom'. I made friends with the other boys in the class and it was great to have someone to play with in the playground. One of the games we played was marbles. The best player was a boy called Stanley. He won most games and would have pockets full of marbles. He would then sell them back to us for two-a-penny.

Mr. Stevens taught the older children but occasionally he would come into our class to see how we were getting on. He would slowly walk up the classroom and look over our shoulders to see what we were doing. If he was satisfied with our work, he would say "Good" as he passed but if he wasn't satisfied, he would take a clump of hair at the back of our ears and twist it. This was really painful and caused you to stand up so that it didn't pull quite so much.

Once he came up behind Stanley and took hold of a handful of hair and surprised the boy. Stanley being taken by surprise, tried to knock the teacher's hand away but he hit Mr. Stevens on the nose instead, making it bleed and causing him to stagger backwards, holding his nose. Stanley took one look at the teacher, and realising what he had done, jumped up onto his desk, which was next to an open window, onto the sill and leapt out of the window and into the playground.

As he jumped, all the marbles in his pocket fell out and scattered all over the classroom floor. It was quite a sight. Mr. Stevens was holding his bleeding nose and all the boys were scrambling around the floor on hands and knees retrieving the marbles and Miss Knight hitting us with her ruler, trying to bring us to order. She had no chance. Not when there were free marbles 'up for grabs'.

When Stanley jumped out of the window, he landed in the playground. When he found his feet, he ran all the way home. His mother unfortunately brought him straight back to school to find out what had been going on, and to find out why her son had arrived back home in the middle of the day. Mr. Stevens escorted them both to his office where I think they must have sorted it all out because before long, he was back in the classroom. The next day he had won all his marbles back!

In the older boys' class there was a boy named Tubby Thomas. He was a bit of a bully. One day he picked on me. I tried to run away from him but he caught me with his arm around my throat. In the confusion, we both tumbled to the ground, with me finishing up on top of him. As Tubby fell, he hit his head on the ground and started to cry.

Miss Knight heard the commotion and came out to see what was going on. She saw me on top of Tubby and assumed that I was bullying him. She pulled me off him and started to smack me on the back of my legs saying that she wasn't going to tolerate bullying in the school.

On the way home from school, I told Gerald about the injustice of being punished as a bully but he laughed and said "I bet Tubby won't pick on you again", and he didn't.

My greatest fear was having to use the outhouse toilet at night when it was dark. Being the youngest, my brothers would tease me about it and tell me that there was a monster living in the wood. One night I had to urgently use the toilet, so I asked someone to come with me but I was told that I must get used to going to the toilet at night on my own. I plucked up the courage to leave the safety of the house and crept outside towards the outhouse toilet. I was frightened of using a torch in case the monster saw me.

I reached the outhouse and sat down, hoping I hadn't been seen. After a while I heard a scraping noise behind me. My heart started to pound as I heard more scraping noises and then there was a horrible howling sound. I was so frightened that I jumped down from the toilet and shot out of the door with my trousers still round my ankles. I ran back to the house shouting for my mum. "Whatever is the matter with you?" asked mum. "It's the outhouse monster" I blurted out. "It's coming to get me!"

At this moment my brother Gordon came into the house laughing loudly and making howling noises. When my other brothers saw me standing there with my trousers around my ankles, they started laughing too. My mum, seeing how upset I was, gave them all a clip around their ears and told them never to frighten their little brother again. I never, ever went in that outhouse again after dark on my own.

It was surprising how well we adapted to life in Furzen Leaze. My mum was the rock for all of us. She would cook a meal out of almost anything on an old iron stove that had seen better days. She also had to do the washing for six of us in an old crock sink. Then she would put the wet washing through a mangle and hang it up to dry on a line outside in fine weather, or on an old wooden clothes horse if it was raining.

I helped her as best I could and she called me her little helper. I would fetch the water in a container from the farm and collect the bread which was delivered to the farm twice a week. I don't really know why but I loved to help her in the kitchen, even when I had to peel the potatoes to go in the pot.

I began to worry about little Sam next door. He seemed to cry a lot. It came back to me what the girl had told me on my first day at school about the Carters eating babies.

I must have been thinking about this one day when I was outside chopping wood for the fire. I stopped chopping and looked up to see why Sam was crying. I was horrified to see that Ruth was dragging the poor little lad through some stinging nettles. I rushed inside screaming for my mum to come outside. I shouted "Ruth is killing little Sam. Come quick!"

When mum came outside she saw Ruth still dragging poor Sam through the nettles and she was outraged. She ran over to Ruth, pushed her away from the child and scooped Sam up into her arms, telling Ruth that she was a very wicked girl.

Mrs. Carter came out of the house and wanted to know what all the fuss was about. Mum told her what Ruth had done and Mrs. Carter smacked Ruth across the head and shouted at her to go inside the house. She told mum she would deal with it, then took little Sam from Mum, gave him a hug and a kiss and then disappeared inside the house.

The next day, mum went to Cirencester. She told me she had to go to see someone there. A couple of days later when I was at the farm collecting some water, I saw some people arrive in a car. Two ladies and a man got out. They looked very posh. The man was wearing a suit and tie and the two ladies were wearing pleated skirts and tweed jackets. The man asked me where the Carter family lived and I pointed to the cottages across the fields. I told him that they lived next door to us and would show them the way across the fields. Before I set off, I filled three more water buckets and gave one to each of the posh people. They all looked at me, confused, until I said "My mum says that you should never come back empty-handed" and they all laughed.

They all seemed very nice people and, as we walked together across the fields, they asked me about my family and if I liked living here. I told them it was a long way to walk to school every day. They also asked me about the Carters, our next door neighbours. I blurted out "They're weird... and they eat babies! My friend at school told me." The lady said that it was just children's silly chatter and not to take any notice.

I wasn't convinced. I was sure that Ruth was trying to kill little Sam.

When we got to our house, I collected up all the buckets of water and took them into the house. Mum was surprised to see so many buckets but when she saw the people outside, she realised that they had helped me to carry the buckets home and said "Richard! Surely you didn't ask those people to carry the water from the farm?" but I said "Why not? You always say we shouldn't come back empty-handed."

Nothing more was said to the posh people. They walked on to the house next door, knocked and went inside. At times, we could hear raised voices through the wall. We walked outside when we saw the visitors coming out of the Carter's house. The lady had little Sam in her arms. The Carters were protesting but the lady said "It's all for the best. Little Sam will be well looked after." As the lady walked past me she said "Sam will be safe now." I watched them walk back across the fields to their car which they'd left at the farm. I couldn't help but wonder what would become of little Sam.

In the evening, when all the family were gathered around the table, mum explained to us what had been going on next door. She said that little Sam was not Ruth's child as we had thought but that he had been fostered by the Carters. She told us she had gone into Cirencester to speak to the Social Services because she had been worried about the child. They told her that the family occasionally fostered children but they would look into the matter as hers was not the only complaint against them. We were all relieved to know that something had been done about it and that they wouldn't be fostering any more children.

It was a hard life living at Furzen Leaze. It was now winter time and it could be cold and wet living here in the middle of nowhere. My brothers, John and Gordon, had to ride their bikes five miles to work in Cirencester six days a week. Gerald and I had to walk two miles to school from Monday to Friday.

Mum knew how to cheer us all up. She insisted that we all should sit around the table for our meals and tell each other what we had been doing that day. I loved to hear John telling us stories about working on the building site. Mum would clip John around the ear if she thought his stories were not fit for our young ears.

The railway line between Cirencester and Kemble ran through the fields near to our house. Gerald and I would go and watch the steam trains going by. We loved to see the trains coming down the line with smoke belching out of the funnel. We'd wave to the driver as the train passed and he would blow the whistle and wave back to us. We waved at the passengers and pulled funny faces. They would laugh and wave back at us.

It was after watching the train one day that Gerald got shot! We were walking back to the house, talking and laughing without a care in the world. John and Gordon were sat upstairs at home. They'd been repairing an old air rifle and were keen to try it out. When we were about fifty yards from the house, Gerald suddenly screamed without warning and shot about two feet up into the air. Then he fell to the ground, groaning and clutching his side. I stood over him too shocked to speak and it wasn't until he undid his shirt that I saw a big red lump appear. He was in a lot of pain and rolling around holding his side.

We couldn't understand what had happened until we saw mum chasing John and Gordon out of the house with the yard broom, hitting them as soon as she got close to them. She was shouting and telling them they could have killed Gerald. I helped Gerald into the house and mum laid him down to have a look at him. He had been hit a with lead pellet which had been fired from the air rifle. The wound had turned into a big purple bruise.

When dad had learnt what John had done, he was really angry and demanded an explanation. John told him with a smirk "Our Gordon bet me a shilling that the pellets wouldn't reach Gerald!" At first dad was speechless. Then he said "You're both mad!" and demanded that they hand over the air rifle. Dad told them they could have it back when they'd learnt to be more responsible.

I shared a bedroom with John and that night I asked him if he had intended to shoot Gerald. He said "Of course not! I was aiming at you."

Chapter Seven

It had been a really cold day and was starting to snow. Mum, me and my brothers were sitting huddled around the fire to keep warm when dad walked into the house. He had a smile on his face when he came out with the two words which we normally dreaded. "We're shiftin'!" he said. We all gave a big cheer and excitedly asked him where we were going to live. Mum hoped it would be better than this place and Gordon chipped in with "Anywhere's got to be better than this dump!"

Dad told us that we would be moving to Cirencester. This was really exciting news. We had never lived in a big town before. Dad had got a job as a whipper-in with the Vale of White Horse (VWH) Foxhounds. The VWH was based in Great Cirencester Park which is owned by Earl Bathurst who lived in a mansion on the edge of the town.

In dad's job as gamekeeper, he had had a lot of contact with the VWH hunt. He had impressed the master of the hounds with his knowledge of hounds and horses, and as a result, had been offered a job as whipper-in.

When the day came for us to move, the farmer very kindly offered the use of his tractor to take our belongings from the house to the farm. We could then load up the removal lorry which would be waiting there to take us to Cirencester. None of us were sorry to leave that house by the side of the wood.

Our new home was number 3 Cecily Hill which was situated on the edge of Cirencester Park. Just a short walk from the Park gates. We all loved our new home. The house had electric light, running water and, best of all, a flush toilet inside the house. Mum was over the moon with her new home, especially when she saw the electric cooker.

I loved living in Cirencester. Everything was on the doorstep. No long walks to school and the shops. I soon made friends with the local lads who were glad to show me around their town.

Living in a big town was all new to me. I had never seen a picture house before. I remember the day I first went inside and was amazed to see the enormous screen. I spent many happy times there with my new-found pals.

My new school was only about ten minutes' walk from home. It was bigger than any school I'd ever attended. It had about two hundred pupils. More than any of my other schools but I soon settled in there. Gerald went to the secondary modern school about half a mile away and my other brothers were happy too because they worked in Cirencester. Gordon was starting to make a name for himself at cricket and was soon playing for Cirencester.

The old house at Furzen Leaze was soon forgotten. Our new life was completely different. Most of all I liked the fact that the shops and school were so close to home.

Cirencester House was the home of Earl Bathurst and his mother, Lady Apsley. They were part of the aristocracy and were acquainted with the royal family. We called them 'the posh people'. Most of the families living in Cecily Hill worked for the big house in some way, either in the house or on the estate. My friend Robert's dad was chauffeur to Lady Apsley and another was the butler to Earl Bathurst. My dad liked his job as whipper-in, his job was to keep the hunting hounds together in a pack when they were out hunting.

At our house in Cecily Hill, we didn't have a garden but we did have six stables for the horses which were used to house the posh people's polo ponies. On polo match days, the grooms would take the ponies up to the Park to the polo field. Polo was a fast and furious game which was played on horseback. The riders had to hit a wooden ball with a polo stick and score a goal.

Hundreds of people would come to watch the game. Many would come in their Bentleys or Rolls Royce cars and, if the weather was fine, they would bring their wonderful hampers full of delicious picnic fare. Some would bring servants with them or their butler to serve the delicious food and champagne. We were shooed away if we got too close.

I joined a group of boys who all lived in Cecily Hill. We had lots of fun and adventures together. Our leader was a boy called Terry. He told us that he was our leader as he was the eldest and the brainiest because he went to the Grammar School. This didn't, however, stop him getting us into trouble. He was always thinking of new ways to get a laugh. One of the things he did was to tie people's dustbin lids to their front door. We would knock on the door and run away. When someone did open the door, the string attached to it would pull the lid off the dustbin and it would clatter on the path, making them jump in fright.

One day, one of Terry's schemes went wrong. He'd read in the national newspaper that sugar had come off rationing. This meant that you could buy as many sweets and chocolate as you wanted without using coupons. Terry told us that all the rich kids would buy them all up and there would be none left for us.

We had no money to buy sweets so Terry had a plan. We would all go to Woolworths on our roller skates and do a raid. We stopped a few yards from the store to discuss tactics. Terry explained the plan to us. He said that we could skate at speed into the store, go around the sweet counter, grab some sweets and skate back out and away before anyone had noticed us.

We were not happy with this plan. It was stealing and if we got caught, we could go to prison. Terry told us it was foolproof and to prove it, he would do a 'dummy run'. We watched him skate down the path and into Woolworths and reappear in seconds with a handful of sweets and a big smile on his face. "I told you it was dead easy" he said.

Convinced it was a good plan, at Terry's command, we set off on our skates and into the store. However, we were in for a big shock. As we skated in, the doors were slammed shut. The staff were waiting for us. We were grabbed by the scruff of the neck and marched out but not until we had been smacked and beaten by staff and customers alike on our way out. Some customers were hitting us with handbags and umbrellas. We couldn't do much about it. We were too busy trying to keep our feet which were still attached to our roller skates. The doors were opened and we were all thrown out of the store onto the pavement outside and told never to come again.

Glad to be outside and nursing our bruised bodies, we skated off down the road. Glad to be free but cursing Terry for coming up with such a stupid idea.

Chapter Eight

It was about this time that I found out that I had another granddad on my mum's side.

Grandad Curtis lived in another part of the town called Watermoor. Mum took me to see him one day. He was a lovely old man who made me so welcome. He lived on his own in a small terraced house and was a collector of cuckoo clocks. He must have had at least fifty. Most of them were in working order and when you walked into the room you were surrounded by the noise of constant ticking of all his clocks.

It was a joy to watch them on the hour when each little door would open. What came out of the doors was not just cuckoos, it also included cats, dogs and all manner of little figures. My favourite was the one that had a man just inside the door who was sat on a toilet. As the door opened, the man would look up with a surprised look on his face.

I would visit Grandad Curtis once a week. Mum and I would sit by his fireside, having tea and cake. He would tell me stories of the time he served as a soldier in the First World War. One day he pulled up his shirt to show me his war wound. It was a scar with a big dent in his side.

My most memorable time living in Cecily Hill was in

1953, the year of Queen Elizabeth's Coronation. To celebrate it, Lady Apsley from the big house decided to have a large pageant in the Great Park and invited all the local people to take part. An enormous arena was built with seating for hundreds of people. All the servants and workers from the Bathurst Estate were called upon to act in the pageant. The theme was 'History Through The Ages'. We would choose a different time in history and wear something from that period and then parade around the arena, passing in front of the 'Royal Box' which was to be full of invited guests. A narrator would then give a commentary on the particular scene and costumed cast as they passed through the arena.

Lady Apsley had costumes made for everyone. Each person taking part would go to the big house to be fitted for their costume. My friend Rob and I were so excited because we were to be spacemen in the grand finale. We would be landing on earth in our spaceship, which was made out of a motorbike and sidecar with a wooden frame built around it in the shape of a flying saucer. The motorbike would be driven into the arena with Rob and I dressed as spacemen in the sidecar, ready to jump out on cue.

At one end of the arena, there was a large holding area where all the cast would gather, waiting for their moment to enter the arena. There was also an enormous marquee erected for the refreshments for everyone after the parade.

On the day of the parade, there were hundreds of people taking part. They came from all the villages from miles around. First of all, the marching bands would enter the arena, playing their rousing music as they marched around. This was followed by the fox hounds, huntsmen and whippers-in (the men who looked after the dogs and horses on the estate). I felt really proud when I saw my dad in his red hunting jacket as one of the whippers-in.

Then the main parade started. In the holding area the cast were assembled. There were roman soldiers to represent Cirencester's roman history, as well as dancers and jugglers to entertain everyone. My brother Gerald was dressed as a street urchin, running around pretending to pick people's pockets.

The narrator sat on a high platform speaking through a microphone, commenting on what was happening in the arena. The audience loved it, clapping and cheering whenever someone new appeared.

The grand finale was when Rob and I appeared as the spacemen in our flying saucer. It was a wonderful sight. Rob's dad, Mr. Miller, had built the wooden frame around the motorbike and sidecar and covered it with a tarpaulin sheet, painting it white with black windows. Stuck through holes in the tarpaulin were two pipes which were to be used to send up the rockets.

Mr. Miller explained to us what would happen. We would roar into the arena on the motorbike and then when we were in front on the royal box, we would jump out and run around with placards saying 'We come in peace' written on them. At this point, Mr. Miller would set off the rockets. This sounded wonderful but in fact the rockets went off in all directions. Some landed in the crowd and another landed in the royal box amongst the VIPs. While all this was happening, Rob and I kept running around with our 'We come in peace' placards, waving them about madly while the narrator was telling everyone that we were under attack! Then we jumped back into the spaceship and were driven out of the arena to a burst of applause from the crowd.

The day finished off with a great big picnic in the marquee. A wonderful finish to a great day of celebration for our new queen.

Chapter Nine

Going to the pictures was a popular pastime. It was a cheap form of entertainment. There would be continuous showings of films, which means that two or three films would be shown continuously over an afternoon and evening, so that people could choose when they wanted to go in. Sometimes the films were halfway through but people would sit right through until they reached the point that they came in. This might mean seeing the end of the main feature and then leaving halfway through it, when it came around again. Sometimes, if people really enjoyed the film they could sit through it all over again.

We would get really absorbed by the action and I can remember once when we were watching Dick Barton, Special Agent, that one of the 'bad men' holding a gun was creeping up on a wounded Dick, the audience started shouting "Behind you Dick!" and carried on shouting it because Dick appeared not to hear them.

I loved the Saturday morning picture show for children. They showed us Walt Disney cartoons, cowboy films and a Flash Gordon serial. At the interval, the manager would invite children who had had a birthday that week up onto the stage. He would get everyone to sing 'Happy Birthday' and then present them with a free ice lolly and a ticket to see a film the following week.

We soon caught onto this 'treat' and me and my friends would go up regularly to get our free lolly and ticket. The manager soon got wise to us when he started to recognise the same faces. I protested and tried to tell him that it was my brother who came up last week, but he wasn't fooled and said "Do you think I was born yesterday?" I remember he gave me a kick up the backside as I was walking off the stage and then a clip around the ear saying "And that's for your brother!"

We loved the pictures but our great passion was swimming. The town swimming pool was about five minutes' walk from Cecily Hill. From 1st May until the end of September, the pool was open every day. A season ticket cost us 7s 6d (37p). This was a lot of money to us in those days. My brother Gerald and I would deliver papers on a paper round or do errands for neighbours to raise the money to go swimming. The pool attendants were Mr. and Mrs. Shaw. They were very kind and let us buy tickets for a half season for 3s 9d (19p).

In the first season, I gained my certificate for swimming a quarter of a mile, which was fifteen lengths of the pool. I was also the first one in our gang to dive off the top diving board which was twelve feet high. The truth of it was, that a group of us were standing on the top board and daring each other to jump off. I was closest to the end of the board when Billy Watson decided to give me a shove and I fell head first into the pool... so, it was a dive.

Running alongside the swimming pool there was a stream, which was three yards wide and about a foot deep. Sometimes, we would take off our shoes and socks and wade into the stream and catch little fish in jam jars. We'd look for Bullheads which were about three inches long with a big round head and which hid under rocks and stones. To find them, you had to lift the stones very slowly and carefully. We used to call them 'Snottygogs'. The star prize was catching a crayfish. They were about four inches long and looked like small lobsters. You had to be very careful how you picked them up because they had long pincers which could give you a nasty nip. We had great fun chasing the girls with them.

One day we managed to catch about six, so we put them into a bucket of water instead of putting them back in the stream. This particular day, our glorious leader Terry said "Let's have some fun and release them into the swimming pool". At first, we weren't keen to do it but eventually Terry brought us round to his way of thinking, telling us it would be a lark. Rob asked how we were going to get the crayfish past Mr. and Mrs. Shaw, the attendants. "Easy" said Terry, "I'll go through the main gate as usual and make my way to the far end of the pool by the perimeter fence and you can pass the bucket to me over the fence." We managed to do this without being seen and then Rob, Billy and I joined Terry by the pool.

We all sat down on a bench with the bucket of crayfish behind us, trying to think of a way of putting them into the pool without being noticed. Then someone said "Let's do the birthday treat". This consisted of being picked up by an arm and a leg and then being thrown into the swimming pool. I knew I shouldn't have asked who was it going to be because the next moment they all looked at me and agreed it should be me because I was the smallest. There was no point in arguing. It had been agreed.

We were instructed by Terry to go to the other end of the pool while he stayed with the bucket of crayfish. Then as we were all shouting and hollering at the other end about it being a birthday treat, I was unceremoniously thrown into the water with a splash and a great cheer from the surrounding crowd of swimmers. At this very moment, Terry emptied the bucket into the pool.

I climbed out of the water and joined the others on the bench at the viewing area. We waited about a quarter of an hour before a man shouted "There's something in the water! I think it's a crab", then someone else shouted "There's another one over here". Girls started to scream and push past other swimmers to get out of the water. Men were shouting and pushing. One girl jumped out of the water trying to remove a crayfish which was firmly attached to the front of her bathing costume. She was so frightened that she tore off her costume and ran naked into the changing rooms. The place was in uproar.

Mr. Shaw came out of his office to see what all the commotion was about and started asking people what had happened to cause such panic. Someone showed him a crayfish on the bottom of the pool, then another. He'd seen enough and guessed who it might be. He knew we were always up to something. He calmed everyone down and said that he would handle it himself. We thought the game was up and he'd come looking for us but he didn't. Just when we thought we'd got away with it, Mr. Shaw called us over and said "When the pool closes tonight, I want you all to report to me. I have a little job for you. If you don't stay behind, I will call the police and they will visit you at home." That was enough to frighten us into staying behind but in the meantime, we turned on Terry for getting us into trouble... again!

After the pool closed for the day, we were called into Mr. Shaw's office and told to sit down and be quiet. He had something to say to us. He told us how stupid we'd been to release the crayfish into the pool. It was also very dangerous. It could have caused panic and people could have been injured. He said he was considering banning us from the pool for the rest of the season but then surprised us all by saying that we were not really bad lads and should learn to respect others.

We felt very ashamed and promised to behave in future, which made Mr. Shaw smile. We thought that was it and stood up to go but he told us that we were not getting off that lightly. He told us that for the next week we would have to stay behind each day to sweep and clean the dressing rooms after the pool had closed. Starting now.

Once again Terry had got us all into trouble. Why did we listen to him?

Chapter Ten

My mum often read the bible but she never went to any of the local churches like most people did. I found out one day that she was a Jehovah's Witness. One day I asked her if I could join the local scout troupe with my friends but she said "No, you can't join". I was surprised at her reaction and asked her why I couldn't join the scouts. "It's against the teachings of Lord Jehovah" she said. "Who's Jehovah?" I asked. Mum thought for a moment and then said "Jehovah is the true God and it goes against his teachings to wear a uniform and go to war." I replied "But I don't want to go to war. I just want to join the scouts." Mum raised her voice and said firmly "You are not joining the scouts, so don't ask again."

My mum had an uncle who lived in another part of Cirencester. His name was Albert but everyone called him Uncle Alb. He lived on his own and mum would cook and clean for him once a week. When Uncle Alb became ill, he asked mum if he could come to live with us. He didn't want to go into a home. Mum found space by moving Gordon into the bedroom that Gerald and I shared.

I liked Uncle Alb. He would tell me stories about his time serving in the army in the Boer War. He was also very generous and would buy little treats for the family. Sadly, after a few months of living at our house, Uncle Alb died.

In his will, he had left mum some money. I don't know how much but mum told me she would put it towards something worthwhile. We all had ideas of what we would do with this money but were disappointed when mum announced that she would use it in the service of the lord. She had heard that some members of her church were going to a convention to be held at a place called Twickenham. She told us that she would like to use some of the money so that she could also attend. I didn't know what to think. I would like to have spent some of the money on going to the pictures. I asked dad what he thought about it but he didn't object to her going to the convention. He said "Well, it's her money."

My brother Gerald and I looked at a map to find Twickenham and I was surprised to see that it was near London which was miles away. I wondered how mum was going to get there, so I asked her. She told me that she had an aunt who lived in London and would ask her if we could come to stay for a while. She wrote to the aunt and got a reply to say that we were welcome to come to stay anytime we liked. Arrangements for the travel were made and I was surprised when mum asked me to go with her. I wasn't interested in the religious side of the trip but I was excited to be going on a train to London.

When the day came for our journey, dad carried our suitcase to the local railway station at Cirencester so that he could see us off on our journey. It was a new experience for me. I had seen trains and even been up close to one but I had never travelled on one before.

As the train pulled out of the station, I looked out of the window to wave at dad and then turned my head to look at the engine bellowing smoke from its funnel. We were on our way!

Our first stop was at Kemble Station where we would have to change trains to get the train to London. On the way to Kemble, we passed close to the house that we'd lived in at Furzen Leaze. I thought about the times that Gerald and I had waved to the train from near our house but never thought that one day I would be travelling on it to London. I called mum to the window so that she could see our old house but she said "No thanks. I saw enough of that dump of a place when I lived there."

I loved travelling on the train to London. As we went whizzing through towns and villages I'd wave to the people I could see. I liked to stick my head out of the carriage window and feel the wind blowing on my face and ruffling my hair. Before long we had arrived at Paddington Station. It was enormous. There were so many people rushing here and there and it was full of other steam engines like ours.

Mum had arranged to meet her aunt at the station. While we were waiting, mum went over to the refreshment stand and bought us two mugs of steaming hot tomato soup. It smelt wonderful and it was the best soup I'd ever tasted.

When we'd finished our soup, we waited on a bench and watched the people walking up and down. It was a world away from where I'd come from. Suddenly out of the crowd strode a lady that mum recognised. It was Aunt Maud. She was wearing a pretty, flowery dress and around her neck she wore a pearl necklace with matching pearl earrings. Looking at her, I thought she must be very rich. Mum introduced us. Aunt Maud was laughing as she said "Joyce. I think we'll have to get him home for a clean-up." I felt embarrassed. I'd got my best clothes on and thought

I looked really smart. Aunt Maud must have noticed my confusion and opened her bag to bring out a mirror so that I could look at my face. My hair was stuck up on end from the rush of wind when I looked out of the window of the train and my face was black from the smoke billowing out of the funnel. We all laughed.

My next adventure was going on the Underground. I'd never seen anything like it but I loved it. I enjoyed going down the escalators into the unknown and the noise of the trains as they rushed into the station made me jump back from the edge of the platform. Aunt Maud explained that you can get anywhere in London by using the underground trains. We got off near Regents Park and continued on foot to Aunt Maud's house. It had large rooms and high ceilings. The walls were covered in lots of paintings. She took us up to our bedroom and told us to make ourselves at home.

Twickenham was a long way from the centre of London so it was agreed that Aunt Maud would come with us to make sure that we caught the right train at the underground station. Then we had to catch a bus to get us to Twickenham Stadium. I'd never seen anything like this stadium. I was speechless. It was so big and there must have been thousands of people there. Mum said that they were all Jehovah's Witnesses and had come to this convention from all parts of the world to pray together.

By the end of the day I was fed up with all that singing and praying. I think Aunt Maud was too. When mum announced she was coming back again the next day, Aunt Maud asked if it would be alright if I stayed at home with her. Mum was reluctant to leave me behind but she knew I didn't really want to go back to Twickenham again and at least I could see some more of London with Aunt Maud, so she agreed.

The next day, after mum had left the house, we set off for Regents Park which was only a five-minute walk away. To get to the park, we had to cross a very busy main road. I'd never seen so much traffic. There were big red double-decker buses and lots of black cabs but once we were in the park it was lovely. We watched the boats on the lake and walked around the gardens filled with beautiful flowers. Best of all was the playground, where I got a chance to have a go on the swings and slide.

When we got back to the house we ate some lunch and then Aunt Maud said that she was tired and needed to lie down for a while. She gave me a jigsaw to do to keep me occupied. I soon got fed up with that and looked out of the window. It all looked so inviting out there, so I crept up to the front door, opened it quietly and stepped outside. I walked up the road gazing at all the wonderful sights around me. I felt excited by my adventure in a big city. The buildings were enormous and made me feel so small. I loved the hustle and bustle of people rushing by and the hum of the traffic. It was never like this back home.

I found myself outside an underground station. It looked familiar. I'd been to one like this before and thought I'd go down and investigate. Inside was a map of the underground system with all the names of the stations. It was full of lines of different colours. Aunt Maud had said that the map was easy to follow. I wasn't so sure but I wanted to see if I could work it out.

My first problem was that I had no money to buy a ticket. You needed a ticket to get through the turnstiles. I saw a gate at the side of the turnstile and watched as the ticket collector let someone go through it, pushing a child in a pushchair. I waited for someone else with a pushchair to approach the gate and then quickly walked up to it. When the ticket collector looked at me, I said "My mum's got the ticket", pointing behind me, and he let me go through. I kept walking without looking back. It had worked, I was through.

I felt really excited as I jumped on the escalator. I arrived at the platform and waited for a train, just as I remembered doing yesterday. I wondered if I would have the courage to get on the train when it stopped in front of me. I did. I rode the train for miles. It was great but I knew I had to get back because I thought Aunt Maud might be getting worried about me. What was I going to tell her? I got off the train and looked again at the map.

I needed to get back to Regents Park. As I looked at the map, a lady came up to me and asked if I was lost. "No" I said "I was just looking for my station." When I told her where I was headed, she said "Good Gracious, that's miles away." She told me which train I needed and that I had to change trains. The map started to make sense and I understood what she was telling me. Feeling pleased with myself, I made my way back to the platform and got on the right train.

Eventually I arrived at my station and made for the turnstiles. Again, I had to be really clever to get through but I'd done it before. I waited until I noticed someone making for the side gate and walked closely behind. I wasn't even noticed.

I walked out of the station and on to Aunt Maud's house. I was really pleased with myself as I skipped along the pavement and waited with a group of people to cross the road. When I got near the house, I started to panic. What was I going to tell her? I couldn't tell her that I'd been riding the underground trains. I had to knock on the door and, as I waited, an idea came to me. I'd tell her I'd been to the park. That sounded much better.

When I told her this, she was very angry that I'd crossed the busy main road by myself and gave me clip round the ear, saying "Don't you ever go out on your own again." I thought I'd got off lightly. If I'd told her the truth, I'd have got more than a clip round the ear!

I think Aunt Maud must have forgiven me because the next day, after mum had gone to Twickenham again, she took me to London Zoo in Regents Park. I loved it. I'd never seen such wonderful animals. There were elephants, lions and tigers. Most of all I liked the chimps. Especially when we watched them having a tea party.

The next day we had to leave to go home. Aunt Maud came with us to Paddington Station to see us off. She gave me a big hug and said "I hope you'll come to stay with me again before too long."

I enjoyed the ride home on the train. It was great to again be roaring through the towns and villages. Once again, I stuck my head out of the window. I knew I'd probably get a black face again but I didn't care. I loved the way the wind blew into my face as I looked at the smoke billowing back from the engine. I didn't want it ever to end but mum told me to close the window because the carriage was filling up with smoke. I didn't really mind. It had been such fun.

When I got home, I couldn't wait to see my friends and tell them about all I'd seen and done. I'd had a wonderful adventure.

Chapter Eleven

It was about this time that my brother John was called up to do his National Service in the Army. We were all sorry to see him leave home but Dad said that it was his duty to serve King and Country. When he came home on his first leave, we were all amazed at how smart he looked in his khaki uniform.

It was while he was home on leave that John met a girl called Sheila. He brought her home to meet mum and dad. Mum liked Sheila straight away - we all did.

Sheila lived on a farm about three miles outside Cirencester. She worked in a shop in the town. To get to work, Sheila had to ride her bike. This was alright on dry, sunny days but not very nice when it was cold or wet. Mum felt sorry for the girl so she invited Sheila to come to lodge with us at Cecily Hill. Sheila was delighted with the offer and said that she would be happy to pay for her keep.

It took a bit of getting used to, having a girl around the house. It meant that us boys could not have a bath in the tin bath in front of the fire but we worked it out to suit all of us. We would have a bath when Sheila was out of the house or have a bath in the back parlour.

I think mum loved having Sheila in the house as, up to that time, it had been an all-male house. Sheila would help mum with the chores and they could talk about what mums and girls talk about.

My brother Gordon was finding it hard to settle. He tried several jobs but he was only interested in cricket. He would go off for trials with the county side. He did, however, play for Cirencester Town cricket side. Gerald was happy and settled at the secondary modern school and made lots of new friends. He would often invite them to our house before we all went off swimming.

My dad seemed happy in his job as whipper-in with the Bathurst Hunt. His job was to keep the foxhounds in a pack and focused on the hunt. If the hunt had had a good day, the posh people would give dad small gifts of money which he would give to mum at the end of the day to help pay the bills.

Sometimes, the hunt would meet in the Great Park. I used to invite my friends along to see the spectacle. A hundred or more horses would be at The Meet, ridden by lords, ladies and all manner of gentry. They looked immaculate in their black jackets and white breeches. In the middle of them all would be the Master of Hounds, the huntsman and whipper-in (my dad). These three were dressed in scarlet jackets and white breeches.

Waiters and valets would walk among them offering glasses of sherry off a tray. We would laugh when we heard them talking in their posh voices. It sounded like they had a plum in their mouths. At exactly 11.00 am the huntsman would blow his horn and move off with the hounds, and close behind were the hunt followers. When they had all moved off, we would help to collect all the sherry glasses. If we were lucky, there might still be some sherry left in the bottom of a glass so we would drink it before the waiters told us to 'clear off'.

We were all quite happy living at Cecily Hill. Gerald and I were happy at our schools and mum said that it was the first time in years that she didn't owe the grocer any money.

But it wasn't to last! Part of dad's job on the days they weren't hunting, was to exercise and look after the hounds (there were about a hundred). It was a practice for the local farmers to supply food for the hounds. They would ring the kennels when one of their animals (horse, cow or sheep) had died. The dead animal would be taken back to the kennels by lorry and skinned, then cut up and put in big boilers, cooked and then fed to the hounds.

One day my dad and a fellow worker were asked to collect a dead cow. On the way there they were involved in an accident. Their lorry swerved off the road and ran into a railway bridge. It was never explained to us why the driver swerved. The driver's injuries weren't serious but dad was seriously injured. He had broken ribs and was knocked unconscious. An ambulance was summoned and dad was taken to hospital.

When dad didn't turn up for tea, we weren't unduly worried. Mum said that we could start tea without him. It wasn't unusual for dad to be late from work. As we were eating our tea there was a knock at the door. Mum asked me to see who was there. As I opened it, I stood open-mouthed with shock. There was a big, burly policeman standing there with a very serious look on his face. I just stood there speechless.

Policemen only came to our house if one of us boys had been up to some mischief. When he asked to speak to Mrs. Pottinger, I told him that she lived next door. Mum heard this and came to see what was going on. Before the policeman spoke, she said "What have you been up to now" and gave me a clip across the ear. The policeman, feeling sorry for me said "No, no, the lad has done nothing wrong. I'm not here about the lad. I was asking for Mrs. Pottinger, the wife of Fred Pottinger." I saw my mum's face turn pale. He went on to say that my dad had had an accident and had been taken to hospital.

As soon as tea was over, mum went to see dad in the hospital. She was relieved to find out that his injuries were not life-threatening but that he would take time to recover, as he was still unconscious.

Dad had been in hospital for about two weeks when we had a visitor at the house. It was the wife of the huntsman, a posh lady from the Bathurst Estate. She didn't knock at the door but just walked straight in, as if it was her right to be there without announcement. Mum and I were on our own when she arrived. I remember she was wearing a long black skirt and matching jacket. She wore high-heeled shoes, a fancy hat and around her shoulders she wore a fox fur.

Mum was taken unawares and bobbed a curtsey. Looking very concerned, the lady told mum how sorry they were to hear of Fred's accident but was certain he would be better soon and up and about again.

As she went to leave, she turned and said that since he wouldn't be fit enough to do his job working with the hounds, they would have to employ someone else as quickly as possible. Therefore, could we vacate the house by the weekend. I saw the look of horror on mum's face. Mum said "How will we find somewhere to live with my husband still in hospital?" The lady seemed unperturbed and said she was sure that we would find somewhere and left.

I looked up at Mum and tried to comfort her. She tried to look brave and said "Like your dad says - something will turn up."

That evening mum, Gordon, Gerald and myself sat around the kitchen table discussing what we were going to do now. Gerald suggested that we might move back to Poulton to live with Granny Pottinger. I suggested that we could live with Grampy Curtis on the other side of town. Gordon suggested putting up a barricade and refuse to move. My mum just said that we were a family and we would stick together no matter what happened.

Well something did turn up. A small house was found for us in Park Lane in Cirencester. Only about 200 yards away from our house.

The house in Park Lane was not as good as the one in Cecily Hill. It was in the middle of a terrace of six houses. It was a three-up and two-down house. The rooms were very small. The front room opened straight onto the street. You had to be really careful when you stepped outside because the cars passed so close to the front door. The back-room downstairs was the scullery. In the fireplace stood a big black range cooker. It consisted of a fire bucket in the centre and a heating oven on either side. On the top were the hot plates. On one wall was a crock sink which had one cold water tap.

Between the two rooms downstairs there was a staircase leading to the three bedrooms. On the upside, the house did have electric light but at the back of the house there was a shared yard in which stood a block of six coalhouses. Next to this block were two toilets. These were shared by the six houses.

None of us liked the new house. We thought it was a bit of a 'come-down' from the house in Cecily Hill. We felt lost and let down. Dad was still in hospital. He wasn't here to sort things out. It had all been left to my poor old mum.

On the day we moved, a lorry and driver turned up to move our furniture. I think the lorry was supplied by the Bathurst Estate. Mum said this had all been arranged so that they could move the new people into our house as soon as possible. It was heavy work moving house but we all pitched in to help load our belongings. Our new house was much smaller and so we had to throw away some of our things. Beds, wardrobes and dressing tables had to be dismantled so that we could get them up the narrow staircase. By the end of the day, we were all exhausted.

After the lorry had gone we all sat in the scullery feeling dejected. Our belongings were stacked up everywhere. I wondered what dad would do if he were here. I'm sure he would sort it all out. Suddenly mum sprang to her feet and said "Right, it's no good us all looking glum. We've been in worse pickles than this. We've got to make the most of what we've got. The first thing we must do is to make up the beds so that we can all get a good night's sleep."

As we boys set about making up the beds, mum decided to ask the neighbours if she could borrow some coal and then started to make up the fire. Then she boiled the kettle to make us some tea. She had a wonderful way of cheering us up when we were feeling down.

Dad was in hospital for another two weeks and even when he did come home, he had to take things easy because he was still so weak.

Mum knew that dad would be out of work for some time, so she took a job doing washing-up in cafés and hotels in the town.

Within the month, dad was feeling stronger and started to look for work. He found a job working at the town's dairy. Dad said the job didn't pay much but he could have as much milk as he liked.

The little house in Park Lane was very cramped. Sheila had one bedroom and Gordon, Gerald and I had to share the little bedroom. Gordon said there was no room to swing a cat. At the back, there was a yard stretching the whole length of the cottages and about seven yards wide. The six coal houses and two toilets stood on the far side of the yard.

There were seventeen men, women and children living in the cottages so you had to be very patient and wait your turn when you wanted to use the toilet. On nice days, some of the men would sit outside the toilets reading the newspapers and talking while they waited for their turn to use them.

On Mondays you could hardly move in the yard because it was washing day. The lines would be full of washing.

We started to settle into our new home. Mum, ever the optimist, told us that things would get better. As usual, dad told us "Summat'll turn up!"

I was pleased that I didn't have to change schools and my friends were still close by. Mum said that money was tight so we would all have to help out. Gordon had a job in the stationers, W.H. Smith. Gerald had a job as a paper boy, delivering newspapers in the town and I earned a little money doing errands for our neighbours.

One day, Gordon came into the house to announce that he was joining the army. "Don't be daft" mum said, "You won't have to go until you're eighteen." Gordon told her "I'm seventeen and if I volunteer I'll get a pound more than if I wait to be called up." He went on to say that if he joined up, there would be more room for everyone at home and one less mouth to feed. He also told mum that he would send some of his wages home to help out too. Mum really didn't want him to go but dad persuaded her that it was right to let him go and told her that it would make a man of him.

Three weeks later, Gordon was in the army. Gerald and I were pleased because there were only two of us sharing a bed and not three but I did miss Gordon. He used to make us laugh when we were all in bed together.

Life soon got back to normal. I was still close to my friends and the swimming pool. I was happy going to Powells School in Gloucester Street. My favourite lesson was drama. The teachers would come up with some good ideas for plays, and we would perform them at various halls in the area, in front of our parents.

One play I can remember was called Widecombe Fair. The setting for the play was a country fair and we all sang the song Widecombe Fair. At the end of every chorus I alone would sing "Old Uncle Tom Cobbly and all". It must have sounded very funny because every time I sang it, the audience would burst out laughing. After the show ended, a man came up to me and insisted on giving me a sixpence. He said he'd never laughed so much in his life before.

I was ten years old when I first fell in love. There was a girl in my class named Ann. I kept smiling at her but she took no notice of me. I told mum and Sheila about her and mum told me that if I wanted a girl to smile at me, I had to find a way to impress her. Sheila suggested that I send her a note together with a small gift. I tried to think of something to give her but I had so little. The only things I had were some German coins which my brother John had given me. He'd been stationed in Germany while in the army and he'd given them to me on one of his leaves.

The next day I plucked up the courage to give her the gift of German coins wrapped up in a note which said

'These coins are worth a lot of money. Do you like me?' Later that day, she sent me a note. I couldn't wait to open it. The note said 'If you send me some more money I will like you'. I looked at her across the classroom and she smiled at me. I thought I must be doing alright so far, so I sent her another three German coins that I had left. I wrapped them up and sent them across the room to her. The note said 'Will this do?' I watched her open the note and look at the coins. She showed them to the girl sat next to her and they both looked at me and smiled. I couldn't wait to get a note back saying that she wanted to be my girlfriend. By the end of the day, no note had come back so I went home sad and confused.

The next morning in class, I glanced across to the girl I loved and she just glared at me. I got my answer in the playground during the morning break. Ann and her friends walked up and surrounded me. I began to feel worried. Ann kicked me hard on my shin and scowled at me as I winced in pain. She said "I showed those German coins to my dad and he says they're worthless because you can't spend them." I tried to stammer out a reply but it did no good. She pointed her finger at me and said "If you think I can be bought with a load of worthless coins, you're wrong." She then kicked my other shin and walked away arm in arm with her friend with their heads together, giggling. I vowed to have nothing more to do with girls ever again. They were trouble.

Top left: John, aged 16.

Top right: Gordon, aged 12.

*Left: The family (l to r)
Dad (Fred), Mum (Joyce),
Auntie Eileen, Richard, Jim,
Gerald with girlfriend Pam
in front of him.*

Bottom left: Gerald, aged 10.

*Bottom right: Richard
(the author), aged 7.*

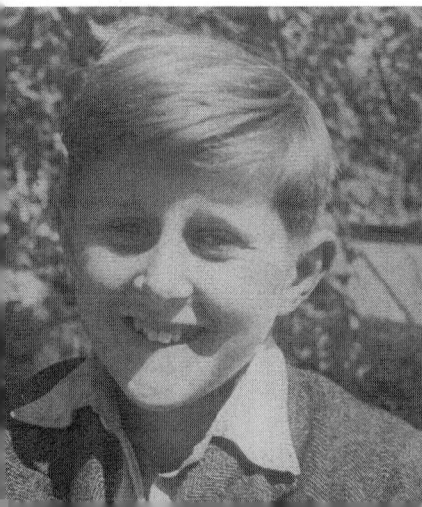

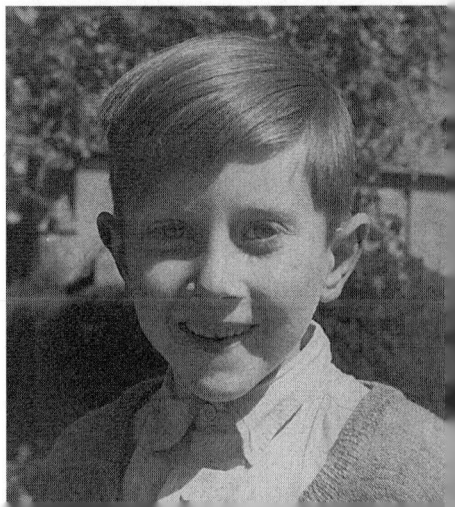

Richard
(the author)
aged 12.

Above left: Richard with his brother Gerald as teenagers.

Above right: The last picture taken of Gordon before he went to Egypt.

Below: John on leave from the Army with Sheila his girlfriend on his motorbike.

Above: Dad (on the left) as huntsman with The Puckeridge Hunt.

Below: The house in Park Lane, Cirencester where we moved after Dad's accident.

Chapter Twelve

In the centre of Cirencester, by the market place, there's a wonderful old church called St John the Baptist. It was built in the 15th Century. The church tower is over 160 feet high and for a small fee the public could climb the staircase to the top of the tower to admire the view.

Our brainy leader Terry had a little brother who we called Shorty. He was nine years old but small for his age. Shorty sang in the church choir and told us that if we paid thruppence each, the verger at the church would take us up the church tower to see the view from the top.

One Saturday morning, our little gang (Terry, Shorty, Rob and me), with thruppence in our pockets, headed for the church to meet the verger who would take us up the tower. When we got there, we couldn't find the verger anywhere. Shorty showed us the door to the tower which was open and still had the key in the lock.

We waited for a while by the open door, thinking that perhaps the verger was on his way but soon we got impatient and Terry said that being as the door was open, we might as well go on up and save ourselves thruppence each. There were mumblings about it being dangerous on our own but Terry said that the verger had probably been called away and he'd left the door open so that we could go on up. The thought of saving our money, persuaded us to follow Terry up the tower.

The stone steps were very steep and narrow. They went round and round a central pillar but we could hold on to the metal rail as we climbed. Halfway up we had to stop to get our breath back. Then we climbed steadily, reaching a door that led us to the top of the tower.

We stood again to get our breath back for a while and then looked around at the battlements. In each corner of the tower was a tall stone pillar, and on each pillar, were ugly gargoyles. Then we looked over the battlements at the view. It was amazing. We could see right to the horizon.

I wanted to see the view from each side and ran from one to the other until I had seen it from all sides. I could see lots of people milling around on the ground like little ants. It was quite frightening being so high but exhilarating too. We started to point out the landmarks. We could see the houses we lived in, our school and the outdoor swimming pool but best of all, we could see Cirencester House and the great park beyond. We stayed there for quite a while, taking in the amazing view.

We had been up there about half an hour when we decided it was time to go back down. We slowly trudged down the steep and narrow staircase in single file and noticed how much darker it was getting. The only light we had, was coming through a small glass window set at intervals in the wall of the tower. Terry thought that someone must have turned the lights off since we had gone up the steps.

We started to feel nervous because we couldn't see our feet. Terry encouraged us to keep a tight hold on the rail and to take our time and we'd be okay. It seemed to take forever to get back down the tower and when we reached the bottom, we were in total darkness. Terry felt for the door handle, turned it but found that not only was it closed but it was locked. Someone shouted "It can't be, try it again". He tried it again but it was definitely locked. We started to panic and shout for help. Shorty started to cry and between sobs he told us it was God's punishment for not paying the thruppence to go up the tower.

Terry kept his cool and felt around the door for a light switch, found it and we suddenly had lights on all the way up the staircase. "Right" said Terry "On my signal, everyone shout help as loud as you can." We did it a couple of times but nobody came. We sat down on the steps with our heads in our hands wondering what to do next. Then Terry came up with another idea (oh dear! Every time Terry had an idea we ended up in trouble.)

He suggested we all went to the top of the tower, look over the battlements and shout for help. None of us wanted to climb up those steep steps again but we didn't have a better idea, so up we trudged. At the top, we had to stop to get our breath before looking over the side to see if anyone was about. We could see people walking around. We waved and shouted and one or two people looked up but they must have thought we were just having some fun so they waved back! So much for that idea.

Then Terry said that one of us must climb onto the battlements so that we could be seen by those below. None of us wanted to do this alone, so Rob and I volunteered and climbed up with our head and shoulders just above the top of the battlements. This must have done the trick because people were starting to gather around and were pointing up at us. They were joined by a policeman who was shaking his fist so we knew we were in trouble. A small crowd of people followed the policeman into the church. This meant that it was likely the door would be opened and we could escape so we made our way back down the steps.

None of us wanted to be the first to get to the bottom because we knew that the first one out would get a clout. Terry pushed me to the front and said "You go first".

We could hear raised voices as we came back down and then the policeman yelled up the steps "Come down here, at once!" We stopped halfway down and froze with fear. The police! We're in for it now. Shorty started to cry saying "We should have paid our thruppence". I knew we had no option but to keep going down and submit to our punishment. I was the first to see the policeman waiting for us. He'd climbed up some of the steps, was slumped against the wall and holding onto the rail gasping for breath. Someone shouted from below "Are you alright Stan?" "No" he said "I'm going to have to come back down." We heard lots of shuffling and groaning and then we started slowly back down.

When we got to the bottom we were met by a very angry, red-faced policeman and a crowd of curious people. One angry lady told us we should be ashamed of ourselves. A man shouted that we should all have a damn good hiding. We all felt very embarrassed that our day's adventure should turn out like this but our saviour turned out to be the verger. He pushed his way through the crowd and started to tell everyone that he'd invited us to go up the tower and had unlocked the door and was waiting for us to arrive but was called away. When he returned, he thought we hadn't turned up, so he shut and locked the door.

The crowd, on hearing this, changed their mood and began to feel sorry for us. They said we had been very brave. Then everyone started to drift off. The excitement was over. We didn't feel brave or excited by our adventure and we slowly drifted off home. Before we had gone far, the policeman came up to us, still red-faced and angry. He said "You were lucky today. Don't you ever go up that tower again without supervision." We promised we wouldn't and made to leave but his passing shot was "I shall be watching you lot!"

As we walked home, Rob and I were blaming Terry for once again getting us into trouble. Terry replied "What are you all moaning about? I've saved you thruppence each."

Chapter Thirteen

I had a cousin, his name was Jim. He was eleven years old, two years older than me. He lived with his mum (my Auntie Eileen) and his elder sister Anne in a village called Frampton Mansell, which was about 4 miles away from Cirencester. Auntie Eileen would sometimes invite me to stay with them for a few days so Jim and I could play together.

To get to their village I would have to catch the Cirencester to Stroud bus. Frampton Mansell was situated on the side of a very steep-sided valley. It was a hair-raising ride on the twisting valley road but I loved it.

Jim and I got on very well and had great times together but at times he got us into trouble. The London to Stroud train line ran along the bottom of the valley. Jim and I would make our way down to the railway line and walk alongside the track to a signal box which stood on a high platform. Sometimes the signalman would invite us in for a cup of tea and a biscuit. We could then watch him pull and push the long handles which he used to change the signals on the track. I loved to watch the giant steam trains with their smoke billowing out of the funnel and roaring past at great speed.

Half a mile up the track from the signal box was a big, long tunnel. Jim and I would walk up to the entrance to the tunnel and look in. One day, Jim suggested that we walk inside but I told him it was too dangerous. I was frightened that we'd be hit by a train. Jim told me it was quite safe because there were places in the tunnel wall where we could stand if a train came. Although I wasn't sure, I didn't want to look like a coward, so I followed him into the tunnel. We walked for about thirty yards. Everything was pitch black. All we could see was the light at the entrance to the tunnel which looked a long way off.

When we spoke, our voices echoed off the walls. I told Jim that we should go back but before he could answer me, we heard the rumble of an approaching train. It was getting louder and louder as it roared towards us. We started to run back the way we'd come but we were knocked over by the blast of wind caused by the train in the tunnel.

We picked ourselves up and hugged each other in fright. We could see the lights of the train and sparks coming out of its funnel. The noise was deafening. The ground started to shake. I was petrified. Then with a blast like thunder, the train roared past. Jim and I just stood hugging each other, transfixed by the sight of the engine and carriages whizzing past us. I looked up to see the faces of the passengers as they flew past at a terrific speed. Then it was gone and the tunnel was silent again. We were left choking on the smoke and soot from the train.

The experience had frightened us to death but we both agreed it had been worth it. We loved it. We walked back up the tunnel and waited for another train so that we could have the experience all over again.

We were going to do it a third time when we heard voices from further down the line, just outside the tunnel.

Two men were running up the line towards us. Jim and I thought we had better make ourselves scarce so we climbed up the embankment, through the perimeter fence and ran home across the fields.

When we got to Jim's house, we were confronted by Auntie Eileen. She looked sternly at Jim and said two boys had been spotted playing on the railway line. Quick as a flash I said "It wasn't us Auntie!" but as she surveyed our black faces and soot-covered clothes her anger grew and she accused us of lying. She told Jim that he should know better. He was two years older than me.

Before she could say any more Jim pipes up "Mummy, it wasn't my fault. I told Richard not to go into the tunnel but he did. I had to go into the tunnel to get him out before the train came." I tried to protest but she held up her hand and said "No more lies. Next time you just listen to Jim." I could see Jim standing behind Auntie with a big grin on his face. I felt so mad but knew it was no good protesting because she wouldn't believe me. One day, I thought, I'll get my revenge.

That day was not long in coming. A few weeks later Jim came over to our house for the day. We went to the Saturday morning pictures which was always good fun. After the show was over and we were all milling around outside the cinema, a cry went up "Fight, fight!"

We looked up to see two lads squaring up to each other. Everyone gathered round to watch. Both lads stood with their fists up, daring the other to strike first. Everyone was egging them on. Suddenly cousin Jim walked up to the two lads and stood between them. He said "Stop this fighting and shake hands!" The crowd went silent. The two boys looked at Jim, looked at each other, nodded and then each landed a blow on each of Jim's eyes. The crowd cheered and hollered (me included). The two lads laughed, shook hands and walked away.

When we got home, mum looked at Jim and asked what had happened. Jim told her that he'd been set on by two boys and Richard didn't help him. In fact, he said I'd run away. Mum said "By the look of those black eyes, you should have run away too." I looked at Jim and smiled. Revenge is sweet!

Chapter Fourteen

My brothers John and Gordon were both in the army so we were not as cramped at Park Lane as we had been before. Gerald and I shared a bedroom and John's girlfriend Sheila had the third bedroom. I think mum was pleased to have Sheila living with us. They got on really well together.

Dad was still working at the dairy but I don't think he liked working there. I heard him telling mum on several occasions that he would like to work with the foxhounds again.

Therefore, I wasn't too worried when he came out with those two words "We're shiftin'!" Dad told us that he had a job with the foxhounds again and that we'd be moving to another house. I felt pleased because this meant that we probably wouldn't have to queue up for the outside toilet at the new house.

When dad said he had a job with the foxhounds, I thought he meant at Bathurst Park where he'd worked before his accident. My heart sank when he told us that the job was with another pack of hounds, somewhere else. Gerald and I spoke as one "Where?" Dad told us with a smile on his face that it was with the Puckeridge Hunt. We wanted to know how far it was from Cirencester. Dad ignored the question and continued telling us that it was the largest pack in the country. He told us very proudly that he would be the 'whipper-in' for the huntsman.

Gerald and I started to get really impatient and asked dad again about the Puckeridge Hunt and if it was far away. He told us that it was in a village called Brent Pelham. We all said together "Where's that?" Dad thought for a moment and then said "Hertfordshire". We all looked at each other because none of us had a clue where that was. I looked at mum. She had that resigned look on her face. She knew that she had to go wherever dad's job took him.

Gerald and I were desperate to know more about Brent Pelham, so we asked dad who told us to look it up on a map. We borrowed a road atlas from a neighbour and tried to find it. It took us some time to find but when we did, we were shocked to find that it was miles away. About 120 miles to be exact. It seemed like the other side of the world to us.

When I got over the shock, I got quite excited about moving to a new house but then it started to dawn on me just what I would be missing. I started to get that feeling of dread when you move schools and have to make new friends. I liked living in Cirencester. We had everything on our doorstep. The swimming pool, Saturday morning pictures and all our grandparents and cousins living nearby. Most of all, I liked my friends.

I asked mum if she could persuade dad to stay but she sighed and told me that dad was determined to make a new start elsewhere. I felt mad at dad. Why does he always keep moving on? My friends' dads don't keep changing jobs like he does. I asked mum about this and she told me that one day, when you're older, you will understand. She told me to think of it as a new adventure. She was sure I would like this new place just as much if I gave it a chance. I wasn't so sure.

I was eleven years old. I felt that I was growing up. I wanted to know why we had to keep 'shiftin'. When I asked Gerald, he just shrugged his shoulders. I wasn't told anything. It seemed that everyone was talking about it but not to me. I only knew the day we were leaving when mum thrust a note for the teacher in my hand which told her which day we would be leaving the school.

My teacher, Miss Reid, read the note and told me she was sorry to see me go. My eyes started to fill with tears. I didn't want to go either. Miss Reid put her arm around my shoulders and told me not to worry. "Everything will be fine" she said. She announced my departure to the rest of the class and some of the boys cheered but most were sorry I was leaving.

This gave my teacher an idea for a geography lesson. She cleaned the blackboard and drew an outline of a map of Great Britain. Then she put crosses and names on the map to show us the position of each main city. She asked each of us in turn, the places we'd visited so that she could mark where they were on the map. Most of these were in the south or south west of Cirencester but none were near Brent Pelham (which is about 50 miles north east of London).

Most of my class mates told me I was lucky to be moving somewhere new. I pretended that I was looking forward to the move but I wasn't. I felt very sad. I really hoped that dad would change his mind but the date was set to 'shift'.

John's girlfriend Sheila who was staying with us was very upset that we were moving. She didn't know how she was going to meet up with John who was still doing his National Service in the army. She talked it over with mum and mum asked her to come with us. I was glad she was coming too. I'd got used to Sheila being around and thought of her as my big sister.

The day of the move came around. A big high-sided removal lorry pulled up outside and everyone helped to load up our belongings. I decided to slip quietly away. I wanted to go to Cecily Hill to see my friends before I left. As I walked up the road, I spotted Terry, Rob and Willy with their swimming towels tucked under their arms. Terry said "Haven't you gone yet?" and laughed. "We're going swimming" he said. I couldn't tell him how unhappy I was that I was leaving and wouldn't be going swimming with them anymore. I felt lost and wanted to go with them but knew that I couldn't go.

I walked back to Park Lane feeling totally rejected by my friends.

When the lorry was loaded and we were ready to leave, I had one last look around our house. It was a dump but I would rather live here than leave Cirencester.

The travel arrangements were sorted out. The driver and his mate, along with mum and Sheila, would travel in the driver's cab. Dad, Gerald and I would travel in the back of the lorry. A sofa had been placed in the back for us to sit on, facing outwards. The top of the rear door had been left open so that we could see out.

I didn't want to leave Cirencester and the life I'd known there. Up to now, all our moves had been just a few miles and it meant that we could still stay close to our relatives so that we could easily visit them.

Nobody came to see us off. The lorry set off and I looked out to see if I could see anyone I knew but I saw no-one.

For the first half an hour, Gerald and I thought it was exciting leaning out of the back of the lorry but the novelty soon wore off and we were glad to sit on the sofa with dad, where we stayed for the next two hours of the journey.

Before too long, the lorry suddenly stopped in a lay-by. The driver came around the back to tell us that we were stopping for a lunch break. We passed down a table and chairs, and also some boxes to sit on. Mum found the food box with some sandwiches which she had made for everyone. The driver set up a paraffin stove on which he set a kettle to make some tea. We must have looked a strange sight, a family sat around eating our lunch in a lay-by.

After we'd finished, we loaded up our table and chairs and set off on our way once more. It took another three hours to get to Brent Pelham. We went through towns and villages which I'd never heard of. We travelled on the back of that lorry for about 120 miles, by which time I had become really tired. The last few miles were down narrow, sunken roads but eventually we reached our destination: The Puckeridge Hunt Kennels.

The driver came off the main road, drove through an open gate and into the kennel yard. We all jumped down from the lorry in high spirits. We were met by a man who introduced himself as Dennis Tennant. He told us that he was the groom who looked after all the horses on the estate. He shook hands with mum and dad before showing us around our new home. As we turned to look at it, we all fell silent.

We didn't know quite what to make of it. The house was constructed completely of wood. Attached on either side was a row of stables. Mr. Tennant opened the door and we all walked in behind him. "Nice in here" he said. "I used to live here until two weeks ago but I now live in a better house just up the road." Mum turned to look at Sheila and said "That makes us feel second-best doesn't it?"

While the lorry was being unloaded, Gerald and I went to look around our new home. As it was built entirely of wood, it blended in with the stables on either side. The front door led into a large room which would serve as our living room and kitchen. On the side wall was a large brick inglenook fireplace. Inside this stood a large Aga cooker which seemed out of place in a wooden building. On the far wall was the door to the scullery and on the other side of the scullery was the door which led to a toilet. There were stairs to the left of the front door. At the top was a small landing, off which were three bedrooms. The inner walls were made of wood panelling.

Mum also had a good look around the place and then announced to dad "You've brought us to yet another dump! It's really just a shed." He ignored this and stated that at least it had electricity. Mum went on to say that he should have looked around the place and checked it over before accepting the job but he replied "It was too far to come". We later found out that Mr. Tennant had taken the house up the road that was really meant for us. Once again, my poor old mum had to sort everything out. At least she had Sheila to help her.

The first thing we did was to get the beds put together. After a long day, we all needed somewhere to sleep. We also felt really hungry so mum and Sheila got the Aga going and cooked us a meal. Finally, we were ready for bed.

The next morning, I got up early and couldn't wait to have a look outside. The kennel yard was quite big. It consisted of our house and adjoining stables. Attached to the stables was a tall building called the skinning shed. On the other side of the yard stood some large wooden buildings. These were the kennels where the hounds were housed. It was like a hotel for dogs. It had several pens to separate the older dogs from the younger ones and the dogs from the bitches. There was a large kitchen to cook the dogs' food and another room containing a feeding trough for the dogs.

Outside, there were several grass paddocks to exercise the hounds. Some of the paddocks contained sheep and deer. Everything was surrounded by a high wire fence to stop any animals escaping. It reminded me of a prisoner of war camp.

Brent Pelham was a village of two halves. The centre was on the top of a hill, where the church stood. On one side of the square was the village shop and post office. On the other side were some large gates leading to the mansion house which was the home of the Barclay family who owned most of the farms and farmland in the area. Half of the village was on the south side and we lived on the north side where The Black Horse pub stood which was opposite the village school.

We named our new home in the kennel yard 'The Shed'. Mr. Tennant, the head groom, had moved out of our house to make way for us. He said that it used to be the tack room where they kept all the saddles and harnesses.

Mum and Sheila made the house more livable. Mum was a 'dab hand' at making do.

Once again, Gerald and I had to go to new schools. I hated it. Mum found out that Gerald had to go to the secondary modern school at a small town called Buntingford which was about 6 miles away. I was only eleven, so I went to the village school at Brent Pelham. Mum took me down the road to the school and introduced me to the headmaster. The school was the usual village school. Two classrooms. One for big kids and one for little kids. I was put in the bigger kids' class. I felt very embarrassed when the teacher, Mr. Grey, introduced me to the class. I had nothing to fear. The whole class wanted to know all about me. I was made very welcome and soon settled in and made friends.

Moving to Brent Pelham was a completely new experience for me. I had got used to living in a town but now I was back to living in the countryside again.

Living in the kennel yard was something quite new to me. I liked to watch the grooms looking after the horses and enjoyed helping to feed and water them.

One day, dad took me over to the kennel block to have a look around. We went through the main buildings and out into a large area where there were hundreds of dogs which were segregated into pens. When I called them dogs, dad sternly corrected me and told me that they were called hounds, not dogs.

I liked the hounds. They stood about two feet high and were quite colourful. Some were white with black patches and others were white with brown patches on them. They had a long tail which stuck straight up in the air. They had friendly faces and I felt safe walking amongst them.

We were approached by, what I first thought was a boy, but soon realised was actually a girl in a pair of boy's trousers. "Can you milk a goat?" she asked. I shyly answered "No". With a smile, the girl said "Come with me and I'll show you how to do it". As we walked, she introduced herself as Maddie Thorpe and told me that her father was the huntsman, adding "He's in charge of everything here."

When we found the goat, Maddie said "Watch me and I'll show you how to milk a goat." I watched her as she stroked and patted the goat and placed a bucket underneath and then worked her hands down and under the goat's belly until she reached the milk sacs. Then she began to pull and squeeze the teats until the milk squirted into the bucket.

When the bucket was half full, Maddie turned to me and said "Right! Now you have a go."

I'd seen a cow being milked before, but never a goat. Feeling a little nervous, I knelt down beside the goat and took hold of the teat but, the goat sensing that I was nervous, turned its head to look at me, then kicked out with its back legs, knocking me backwards and spilling the bucket of milk all over the floor. Maddie burst out laughing and said "You must be gentler with her." I was determined to keep trying to get it right. After a few more kicks from the goat, which I managed to avoid, I eventually got the hang of it.

Maddie showed me around the paddocks near the kennels. There were deer, sheep, geese and goats roaming around the fields. She told me it was necessary to keep these animals near the hounds so they got used to seeing them and didn't chase them while out on a hunt. Maddie and I became good friends.

The view from our kitchen window was a bit shocking at first. We looked out onto the skinning shed. Mum, Sheila and I hated it. Realising how I felt about this, one day dad asked me to go with him to the skinning shed to see what happened there. Inside the shed was a man skinning a cow. I was reluctant to go inside but dad said "If you're going to be a hunting man, you have to get used to it."

The man skinning the cow was called Mr. Bell. He was the kennel man and it was his job to feed and look after the hounds. Seeing me standing by the door, he called out to me "Come on in young Rich and I'll show you what it's all about." I watched him using his skinning knife as he cut off the cow's coat. He told me that it was called the 'hide' and that it was important not to damage it because it would be used to make leather goods and was therefore worth a lot of money. After he had removed the hide, he threw it to one side and covered it in salt, telling me that the salt would preserve it.

Next, Mr. Bell turned his attention to the cow's stomach which he cut open with his skinning knife. All the contents of the stomach poured out which was horrible. I wanted to go but dad insisted that I stayed. Mr. Bell explained that the contents were called offal which would be used as fertilizer. Then the rest of the cow was cut into pieces and loaded into a wheelbarrow.

After the wheelbarrow had been filled, dad and Mr. Bell wheeled it into the kennel building where it was thrown into an enormous vat, about four feet high and six feet wide, before lighting a gas burner underneath so that it could be boiled up and cooked for food to feed the hounds.

I got used to the skinning shed in time and often saw all kinds of animals (cows, sheep and pigs) being taken into the shed and later wheeled across the yard.

One thing I never did get used to, was seeing the old work horses being 'put down'. Mr. Bell would lead the trusting old horse into the shed, where he would use a special gun to shoot it. It reminded me of Old Bon, the horse I had loved when I was younger. I wondered if this was his fate too.

One night we had a wonderful surprise. It had been raining hard when we went to bed. Before we could settle down to sleep, there was a loud knocking on the front door. Dad got up and opened the door to find two men standing there, soaking wet from the rain. One of them said "Any chance of bed and breakfast?" Then the man looked up into dad's face and grinned. It was then that dad realised who it was. "Well I never" he said, "it's our Gordon!" Dad shouted up to us "Come on down everyone. It's our Gordon."

We all came rushing down the stairs, nearly falling over each other in our haste to be the first to give him a hug. Mum got there first and flung her arms around his neck and hugged him. We pulled them into the room and they sat down at the kitchen table. Mum put the kettle on the stove and asked Gordon and his friend if they were hungry. "Starving!" said Gordon.

Then he introduced us to his best army buddy, Bob. They had three days leave from the army and Gordon thought it would be great fun to see if he could find out where we were living now. They'd been travelling all day and asking people the way to Brent Pelham. By the time they had arrived in the village, it was dark and raining so they knocked on doors to ask if anyone had seen a new family arrive in the village. Eventually they found us. Gordon said that they had a shock at one farmhouse when the farmer came to the door with a shotgun, threatening to shoot them because he thought they were after his chickens.

Mum made them tea and sandwiches. When they'd finished eating, mum could see that they were tired so she told them to go upstairs, get out of their wet clothes and they could sleep in Rich and Gerald's beds. Gerald and I shot a look at mum. She laughed and said "You two can sleep on the sofa tonight." We didn't mind really. We were just glad to have Gordon back with us again, even if it was only for a day or two.

The next day Gerald and I couldn't wait to talk to Gordon and find out about his time in the army. The first thing Gerald wanted to know was "Have you shot anyone yet?" Gordon laughed and said "No, the army wouldn't trust us with a gun." Bob told us that their job was to build bridges and to keep the army on the move. Gordon told us that he spent most of his spare time playing cricket.

The reason for the three-day leave was because Gordon's regiment was about to go overseas. Mum looked worried and said "I hope it's not anywhere dangerous." Gordon laughed and told her they were being posted to Egypt and the only thing they would be bothered by would be the flies. Dad, who had been quietly listening, perked up when he heard Egypt being mentioned. "You be careful out there" said dad. "There's some bloke called Nasser who's trying to kick us out." "Don't worry" Gordon said "we'll sort him out!"

For the next couple of days Gordon and Bob got spoilt something rotten. Mum made them cakes and tea and fussed over them. Gordon said he loved being in the army. He was being trained to be an electrician which would give him a good trade when he left the army.

It was lovely having my big brother back with us again but time went quickly and soon his leave had come to an end. On the Tuesday morning, Gordon and Bob caught the double decker bus which came through the village on its way to Bishops Stortford, our nearest large town about ten miles away. From there, they could find their way back to the army base. We all went with them to say goodbye. There were lots of hugs and kisses and then the two pals boarded the bus. As it pulled away, I ran after it.

Gordon was stood on the back plate with a big grin on his face, urging me on to keep up with the bus but it speeded up and I was left behind with tears running down my face. I would forever see him in my mind's eye, grinning and waving goodbye as he stood on the platform at the back of the bus. Little did I know that it was to be the last time I would see Gordon.

After Gordon and Bob had gone, I went back to school. I told our teacher Mr. Grey about my brother's visit and how he was on his way to Egypt. My teacher said "Ah,

Egypt. Do you know where it is?" I didn't, so it was a good excuse for a geography lesson. Mr. Grey unfolded a large map of the world and attached it to the blackboard. Then he pointed to Egypt. He told us about the Suez Canal and how it was a vital link between the Mediterranean Sea, the Red Sea and beyond.

He went on to say that the British Army was stationed at the Suez Canal to protect British interest there and that my brother would be part of that army. This made me feel really proud of my brother Gordon. Mr. Grey said that we would review the situation from time to time to see how Gordon was getting on, protecting the British Empire.

A few days after Gordon's departure, dad came home with a surprise for me. He brought a little dog into the house and said "This little fellow needs a good home, so I am giving him to you to look after." I was over the moon with my little dog and fell in love with him there and then. He was light brown with coarse hair and we called him Titch because mum had said he was a little titch when she first saw him.

Dad told us that Titch could never have been a show dog because his legs were too long for his body and so the breeder was going to put the dog down. Dad said that as soon as the dog had settled down, he would teach me how to train him.

Over the next few months, dad showed me how to train a dog. He told me that you must be strict but kind and to get the dog to trust you. It wasn't long before I could get Titch to come to me when I called him and to sit down by my heel.

Chapter Fifteen

My unhappy feelings of leaving Cirencester began to fade. I started to enjoy living in the 'shed'. I had made a good friend in Maddie, the huntsman's daughter. For a girl, she was alright. She could climb a tree nearly as good as me. She lived in a big house just outside the kennel yard. Every day she would get me to help her with the goat and we would both help Mr. Tennant, the groom, to feed and water the horses.

We would go over to the kennels and watch our dads working with the hounds. Maddie's dad told us that there was a strict breeding programme with the hounds. The family trees went back to 1725. They had to train the hounds to hunt as a pack. They did this by shackling a young hound to an older and more experienced hound.

The village shop and post office were a mile by road or half a mile if you took a short cut across the fields. It had become my job to go to the shop for the provisions we needed. The shop was run by a nice couple, Mr. and Mrs. Tilcot. A local girl called Shirley helped them in the shop. Most days when I got home from school, mum would ask me to go down to the shop. This amused me because the shop was on top of a hill, so I told her that she should say "up to the shop" but she would say "that's right, down to the shop". I gave up.

Every time I went to the shop, I would take my dog Titch. He loved to come with me. I taught him to walk on his hind legs. When we were in the shop, I would click my fingers and he would get up on his hind legs and walk around the shop. This made people laugh and clap their hands. He was rewarded by being given a bacon rib bone.

We had only been living in the 'shed' for about two months when things changed again. Dad walked into the house and spoke those two dreaded words again. "We're shiftin'" he said. We all looked at him in horror. Before anyone could say anything, a smile came across his face and he said "We're moving to a better house just up the road."

He told us that Mr. Tennant, the head groom, was leaving the area which meant that his house would be empty. The news pleased mum and Sheila because they hated living in the kennel yard. I was sorry to see Mr. Tennant go. He had been very kind to me; I used to love helping him to feed and water the horses and to change their bedding.

The new house was outside the kennel yard. It was about 100 yards up the road. It was semi-detached and had three good-sized bedrooms. Two were on the first floor and the third was up a second staircase, inside the loft. On the ground floor, there were two rooms, one of which had a 'range' fireplace. The house had a nice front door with a large porch. Just inside the door, on the left, was an inside toilet and a bath. At the back of the house there was a door leading to a small kitchen with a crock sink. Mum's face lit up when she spotted the modern electric cooker. When you walked through the kitchen, there was another door which led back into the room with the range. Mum loved the house and said that she would make it nice and cosy to live in.

On the day of our move to the new house, we realised that we had nothing to transport our things up the road. We had to carry everything ourselves. Maddie came to help us and so did Mr. Bell, the kennel man. We used the groom's 'mucking out' wheelbarrow for our small things.

It took us all day to move our things, including the heavy furniture like mattresses, chairs and sideboard, even though it was only just up the road, but we didn't mind the hard work. We had got a better house to live in.

At the front of the house there was a large vegetable garden. At the side was a large grassed area with two fruit trees. One apple and one pear tree. At the back of the house we had another garden. Here we found a chicken house and coup with chickens. Dad had bought them from Mr. Tennant, who was happy to sell them because he couldn't take them with him to his new job.

We all settled well into our new home. Sheila had the bedroom looking over the front garden and mum and dad had the one that looked over the back garden. Gerald and I had the bedroom on the top floor. We thought it was great fun going up two sets of stairs to go to bed. The room felt like our special den.

I was happier now that I had made friends in the village. In the house next door lived the Paisley family. They had a son called John who was the same age as me. He was full of fun and was always getting into mischief. A bit further down the road lived the Bennett family who had three sons. The eldest son, Albert, became Gerald's best friend. Then came Roger, who was six months older than me. We were the best of friends. The youngest son was Andy.

I enjoyed my time at the village school. We all liked our teacher, Mr. Grey. He had an easy-going way of teaching. He made things interesting to learn. It was here that I at last got to grips with learning our times tables (1-12). On the wall was a list of all our names. By the side of each name were twelve boxes. One for each of our tables. As we recited each one in turn, Mr. Grey would tick a box if we got it right. We felt so proud when all the boxes were eventually ticked.

The boys in the class wanted to know about my brother Gordon who was in Egypt with the army. They wanted to know if he had been in any battles and if he had shot anyone. Just to spice it up, I would tell them that he was fighting battles every day, which wasn't true. In the letter he sent us from Egypt, he told us that there was nothing much to do and that he was bored. He said that it was even too hot to play cricket.

There was a girl in my class called Wendy Burns. She was ten years old with long dark hair which was tied in plaits down her back. She would tell us wonderful stories, mostly about animals. Mr. Grey would ask her to stand up at the front of the class to tell us her stories. He said that it was the best way to keep us quiet. Wendy inspired my interest in reading. She told me to think of something I was really interested in and read about it. She lent me a book called Black Beauty by Anna Sewell. It's the story of a young horse growing up and being sold to new owners. Some good and some bad. It reminded me of always having to move on. I will always be grateful to Wendy for giving me inspiration to read and to write of my experiences.

Wendy's dad was the local blacksmith. I would go with my friends to his forge in the village on cold days and watch him work. We would see him putting shoes on the horses. He would ask one of us to put the kettle on the hot forge while he worked and we would all have a lovely hot cup of tea.

We would take it in turns to use the bellows to pump up the fire until it was white hot. It was fascinating to watch him take a length of metal, put it into the fire until it was red hot and then put it on the anvil to pound it and make it into a shoe for the horse. When it was ready, he would carry it over to the horse with a long pair of pincers and pick up the horse's hoof, put it into place and nail the shoe onto the hoof.

I wondered if it hurt the horse but Mr. Burns reassured me that it didn't hurt. He said "Horses are like us. They love to have a new pair of shoes."

My friend Maddie became ill and was confined to bed for a while. Her mum asked me if I would milk her goat. I wasn't very keen. I remembered being kicked up in the air by it the last time I tried but I was persuaded to give it a try. I went to look for the pail and then went in search of the goat. When I found her, she looked at me with suspicion. I said "Look here goat! Don't give me any trouble."

I ran my hand along her back and worked my way down to her teats. I knelt down beside her and slowly started to milk her. Soon I had a good two pints of milk in the pail. I stood up and gave her a friendly pat on her bony back. I said "I can't keep calling you goat, so I'll call you Bess."

I took the milk back to Maddie's mum. She smiled at me and told me that I could keep it, so I took it home. Mum was really pleased when I showed her the milk. She showed me how to strain it through gauze and then leave it to cool.

When Maddie was well again, she told me I could keep Bess and look after her. I would milk Bess before I went to school and again when I came home. It meant that the family had free milk every day. Mum would make lovely creamy rice puddings with it which became our favourite.

There was not a lot of choice of work for the females of the village where I lived. Both the girls and the women would work on the land or in the stables. Most of the other women would work in Cambridge 30 miles away and would catch the bus as it came through our village at about 6.30 in the morning. Many of them worked in factories and wouldn't return until about 7.30 in the evening. Sheila got a job at Pyes factory in Cambridge which made radios.

She would catch this bus every day, so that in the wintertime she would never see Brent Pelham in daylight.

My thoughts of Cirencester began to fade. I started to enjoy living in the countryside. I was happy at the village school and soon made new friends.

I liked to go 'down the shop' for mum. I only had to pick up the shopping bag and my dog Titch would jump up and wag his tail, ready to come with me. On the way to the shop, I would often be stopped by neighbours who would know where I was going and ask me to buy them things from the shop. They would always give me a little extra money for myself and make a fuss of Titch, who couldn't wait to get to the shop and do his little dance to earn himself a bacon bone.

Chapter Sixteen

It was 19th July 1955. I had just finished tea and was on my way to play with friends. When I got to the garden gate, I saw a man standing there. It was Mr. Tilcot who worked in the village shop and post office. I thought it was strange seeing him standing there because he hardly ever left the shop. I smiled and said hello but he looked at me with a sad look on his face and said "Hello young Richard, is your dad around?"

My heart sank. I thought I was in trouble. Everyone called me Rich except when I had done something wrong and then it was Richard. I was tempted to say that dad wasn't around but thought better of it and said "Yes, he's in the house." He turned away from me and slowly walked towards the house. I thought I'd better 'scarper' just in case I was in trouble. Dad could be a bit of a 'loose cannon' at times.

I ran off to play cricket with my friends. When I came back a few hours later, dad was sat on a box under the apple tree in the garden. I knew something was wrong by the look on his face. It wasn't anger but sadness. He also had no 'fag' in his mouth which was unusual. He only stopped smoking to eat his meals. When he saw me, he got up off the box and came over to me with an anguished look on his face. He simply said "Gord's dead!"

At first it didn't register in my mind. I had expected him to tell me off for something I'd done wrong but suddenly realised he was talking about my brother Gordon. I looked at him bewildered. "No, he can't be" I said. "We only had a letter off him a few days ago."

He pulled me to him and in a soft voice said "I'm sorry Rich but Gordon has been killed." My legs turned to jelly and my mind was in turmoil. I didn't want to believe him. I pulled away from him, stumbled and ran into the house to find mum. She would tell me that it wasn't true.

I found her sitting on the sofa. Sheila had her arm around mum and was comforting her. I saw that mum was sobbing and knew then that it was true. Gordon was dead. I jumped onto the sofa and hugged mum. Gerald was sat nearby looking upset and bewildered. He joined us on the sofa and we all huddled together while the tears flowed.

Everything seemed unreal. I couldn't come to terms with the death of my brother. Gerald and I went to bed that night. We shared the same bed and just hugged each other. I had a pain in my chest that twisted and turned. My heart was breaking. I must have eventually fallen asleep and when I woke up it was morning and Gerald had gone.

I got up and went down the attic stairs to mum's bedroom where mum and Sheila were sat on the bed. Mum saw me and called me over. She put her arms around me, held me close and said "You must be very brave". I didn't want to be brave. I just wanted her to tell me that it was all a bad dream.

Sheila told me to go downstairs and have some breakfast. When I went into the kitchen, dad and Gerald were sat at the kitchen table. Nobody said a word. I went over to dad for a hug but as I walked towards him he looked up with a sad look on his face. He was lost for words and, just for something to say to break the silence, he told me to go and milk the goat. "You must milk her" he said "or she will be stressful and in pain." I'd forgotten about Bess. It didn't seem important any more. I found the pail in the kitchen and walked out of the door followed by Titch.

I found Bess, knelt down and started to milk her. When I'd finished I sat on the grass and welled up with tears. Bess came over to me and gave my arm a nudge and gave a couple of muffled bleats. Titch put his paw on my leg and they both looked at me. They seemed to sense my distress which comforted me.

Dad insisted that I went to school as usual. He said that it would take my mind off Gordon. I had a big hug from mum and then set off for school.

When the bell sounded, we were all called to class. I sat down at my desk and felt everyone's eyes on me. I didn't know if anyone knew about Gordon. Mr. Grey called the class to order and then said in a soft voice "I have some very sad news to tell you." He paused for a while and I could feel the pain in my chest again. Mr. Grey carried on "Richard's brother Gordon who is serving in the army in Egypt has been killed."

There was an audible gasp around the room. I could feel myself welling up again. Mr. Grey went on to say "We must all help Richard to get over this tragedy. I don't want anyone asking him any silly questions. We don't yet know any details about how his brother died." However, boys being boys took no notice and the first question I was asked was "Was he shot?" I was too upset to answer and anyway we didn't yet know how Gordon had died. The telegram just said that he was killed in an accident and that more details would follow.

The army enquiry into Gordon's death a few weeks later had found that it had been due to a terrible accident. Gordon was an electrician and on the day he died, he had been working on some large electric fridges. Something had gone wrong and he had been electrocuted and couldn't be saved.

Rumours were going around the school that he was a war hero and had died while trying to save his fellow soldiers in battle and was to be awarded a medal. I should have told them the truth but it made me feel better if they thought he was a hero.

Gordon was buried in a military cemetery in a place called Fayed in Egypt. We were sent photos of his comrades carrying the coffin to his last resting place.

As it was a military tradition, his army friends had auctioned off Gordon's personal possessions. This was to raise money to send home to mum and dad. Mum had a round, brass mirror made with the money they sent. She hung it above the fireplace and every time we looked in it, we thought of Gordon.

Chapter Seventeen

My time was coming to an end at the village school which would soon be breaking up for the summer holidays for five weeks and I would be going to another school. I soon learnt that this was not a time for playing and idling my time away. We were expected to work on the local farms.

All the local farms were owned by the Barclay family. They were an old military family, and had been for years. At the head of the family was the old Major who lived in the big mansion house in the centre of the village. The Major could be seen most days walking around the village and at the kennel yard. He was a kind and polite man who would always ask how you were when he met you.

He had a little dog that went everywhere with him. The dog was a border terrier the same as my dog Titch. The Major told me that Titch's legs were too long for a border terrier. I felt a bit 'put out' by his comments, so I said "I bet you a shilling that Titch could outrun your dog." The Major laughed and said "You're a cheeky rascal!" but put his hand in his pocket and brought out a shilling and gave it to me. "That's for your cheek. I can see that I will have to keep an eye on you" he said and walked off down the road laughing to himself.

The Major's son, Captain Barclay, was a different kettle of fish. He would roar round the lanes in an old Land Rover and, if he saw you, he would screech to a halt and demand to know what you were doing. If you said "Nothing!", he would rant and rave at you and threaten to put you on a charge for idleness. I soon learnt to tell him that I was on an errand for my mother.

The summer holidays were not a time to laze around. The harvest was in full swing and all the kids working on the farm were expected to help out. We loved it. We could earn a fortune picking potatoes and peas. We got paid one shilling (5p) for a bag of potatoes and three shillings (15p) for a bag of peas. My best ever day was nineteen bags of potatoes in one day, earning me nineteen shillings (95p). I thought I was the richest kid in England, until my mum took the money off me to help pay for a new school blazer for the big school which I was to attend after the holidays.

I loved working on the farm and helping to get in the harvest. There was so much to do in a short time. The Barclay farms had enormous fields of wheat, barley and oats, which would all become ripe at the same time. Therefore, it was 'all hands to the pump'.

Most of the work was done with big wide-bladed combine harvesters. The harvester would sort the grain from the straw. Then the grain would be thrown to the back of the machine. It was then stored in a big storage bin and when it was full, it would be transferred to a tractor pulling a high-sided trailer which would be used to take the grain back to the farm where it would be stored in enormous storage silos.

There were still one or two farms which harvested in the old way using binders. These would cut the corn, bunch it together into sheaves and then throw them out of the back of the machine. Instead of using a tractor, a horse was used to pull the binder. We would follow behind the binder, picking up the sheaves and stacking them in bundles of eight or ten, ready to be picked up later.

You were deemed to be big enough to drive a tractor if, when sat on the seat, you could reach the control pedals with your feet. I soon learnt how to make the tractor stop and go. My job was to drive it between the sheaf stacks, stop at each one and wait for the farm hands to load the sheaves onto the trailer. When the trailer was full, I would drive across to a corner of the field, where the sheaves would be unloaded and made into big ricks. While my trailer was being unloaded, another lad would be having his trailer loaded up.

Having young lads like me driving the tractor left the men more time to do the heavy work. My friends and I loved helping the men. It made us feel very grown up. When we had a break, the men would tease us about our driving but we didn't really mind. We felt proud of our work, especially when the farm manager came over to us and paid everyone their wages. I earned one shilling (5p) an hour.

All too soon the summer holidays came to an end and I had to think about going back to school. Myself and about eight others would be going to the big school at Buntingford six miles away.

Up until now, I had always dreaded starting a new school because it always came after another 'shift' but this time it was different. This was a natural progression to a bigger school where I would already know children from my village.

My elder brother Gerald would not be going back to school. He was now fifteen years old and it was time for him to join the 'working world of the grown-ups'.

The school bus had already picked up children from two other villages by the time it arrived in our village at about 8.15. It would then go on to two more villages before arriving at Buntingford School just before 9.00.

The school had about four hundred pupils who were split into four grades according to age. There must have been about a hundred pupils starting in the first grade like me. First of all, we were assessed as to which class we would go into: A, B or C, depending on ability. I was amazed to find that I was in Class 1A.

It was great fun finding our way around the school. Different classrooms were used for different subjects. Outside was a cricket pitch, two football pitches and a full-sized running track.

The first thing we learned was not to upset the Fourth-Year boys. They called us 'runts' in the First Year, and if we were cheeky to them, they would catch us, stick our heads down the toilet and pull the chain.

I found that this first year was a time of wonder. We were introduced to subjects like woodwork and metalwork which I loved. The school had big gardens where we would learn how to grow all kinds of produce. We also had to look after the pigs and chickens. This was great fun but what we loved most of all were the games of football. We would have a game at every opportunity. We played at every break and dinnertime and teams would number up to twenty a side.

I was very happy when I heard that we were going to have swimming lessons at the local pool. I was amazed to find that I was the only one in my group who could actually swim. The pool attendant would put a rope across the pool to prevent anyone drifting into the deep end.

Everyone enjoyed splashing around as well as the lessons but I got bored and wanted to go into the deep end. Our teacher, Miss Harris, refused to let me but I was determined to do it and when nobody was looking, I walked around to the deep end where there was a high diving board. I climbed up the steps and walked out onto the diving board. When my classmates spotted me, they started cheering and daring me to jump. My teacher went ballistic! She demanded that I come down at once. I did. I ran along the diving board and jumped off the end.

As I plummeted down, I pulled my knees up to my chest. As I entered the water, an enormous wall of water shot up and cascaded over everyone. I didn't surface straight away but swam along the bottom of the pool. The attendant was horrified when he saw that I didn't come straight back up. He thought I was in trouble and dived into the water, swimming down to where I was near the bottom and started to grab my arm and pull me up to the surface. He swam still holding on to me, to where my teacher, Miss Harris was standing at the side of the pool. She pulled me up out of the water and slapped me across the head, "You're a naughty boy! Don't you ever do that again." I didn't know what all the fuss was about. I had done it lots of times in Cirencester Baths.

That first year at the big school seemed to fly by. I made lots of new friends. We played football, cricket and, new to me, athletics. The only down side was the school bus. The conductress was a big, fat lady with a 'bulldog' face, and I don't think she liked kids. She would make all the girls sit on the back seats and the boys on the front seats so that she could keep an eye on us.

She insisted we call her Mrs. Rattle but behind her back we called her 'The Rattlesnake'. The pick-up point for the bus was in the centre of the village, near the church. Five of us lived on the edge of the village about a mile away. The bus went right past where we lived but rain or shine The

Rattlesnake would not allow us to get on or off the bus near to where we lived. She insisted that we walk to the church.

However, the day of reckoning arrived one day on our way to school. A few of the boys were doing their best to annoy her. She walked up the narrow aisle between the seats to sort us out and grabbed one of the boys by the ear and was just about to give him a slap when the bus driver braked suddenly and she fell between the seats. A great cheer went up but then we went quiet when we realised that she was stuck fast and couldn't get up.

We shouted for the driver to stop the bus and he slowed down and stopped at the side of the road. The driver left his cab and came up the aisle to see what was happening. When he saw that she was stuck fast, he tried to pull her up by her arms but it was no good, she wouldn't move. Every time he pulled her arms, she cried out in pain. "We need help" the driver said. "The school is only just up the road so we'll ask for help there." The driver went back to his seat, started up the engine and drove off towards the school.

The swaying and bumping of the bus caused Mrs. Rattle some stress but my friends and myself started to snigger. One of the girls came forward and said "Don't laugh at her, that's nasty". The girl's name was Wendy Burns, the blacksmith's daughter. She was the one who used to tell us lovely stories in class when we were at the infant school. Wendy clambered over the seats and got as close as she could to Mrs. Rattle and held her hand, telling her not to worry because help would come soon.

The bus stopped outside the school gates and the driver ran into the school. He returned a few minutes later with the caretaker and a teacher to assess the situation.

Mrs. Rattle was stuck fast so the caretaker suggested taking some of the seats out and went back into the school for his toolbox. With the help of the driver, the caretaker was able to unbolt the seats from the floor of the bus. With some difficulty they managed to lift the seats and take them out through the doors of the bus.

In the meantime, an ambulance had been called. When it arrived, the crew managed to lift Mrs. Rattle up and out of the bus with the help of the driver and caretaker. Poor Mrs. Rattle was crying with pain as she was lifted into the ambulance and taken off to hospital.

We heard later that she had broken her arm and badly damaged her shoulder. She would be off work for some time. At this announcement, all the boys who travelled on the bus cheered.

There was a lad in our village called John Foxall. He was born on the same day as me, 3rd September 1943. John was a bit different from the rest of us. He had something wrong with his bones. He had enormous feet and a 'hump' on his back. He also had a large head and a big, wide mouth, especially when he smiled, which he did often. He had a great sense of humour. We called him Gruffy because he had a great mop of black, unruly hair. Gruffy had a record of which he was very proud. He'd had the cane more times than anyone else in the school. He also got me the cane once. It was all to do with the fire alarm.

Mr. Wheeler, our headmaster, informed the school one day in assembly, that we would be having a fire drill so that we would know what to do in case of a real fire. This involved leaving the school building in an orderly fashion and congregating on the playing field.

We did this a couple of times before the headmaster was happy that we were doing it right. He then said that we would be having an unannounced fire drill sometime during the term.

A few weeks later, Gruffy and I were walking down one of the corridors when we were confronted by our Maths teacher, Mr. Evans. "I've got a job for you two" he said. Further down the corridor was one of the 'break glass' fire alarms. Mr. Evans found it and told us to break it, to sound the fire alarm. "But Sir" we said, "There's no fire." He answered us with "Do as you're told."

Now you didn't disagree with Mr. Evans. He was a large man with a shock of red hair. Gruffy looked at me and grinned saying "This could be fun." He took the little hammer next to the box and broke the glass.

Immediately, all the fire alarms went off in the school. Gruffy and I looked at each other and then at Mr. Evans. "What do we do now?" I asked Mr. Evans. He grinned at me and said "If I was you, I'd make yourself scarce."

In the next few minutes, the whole school (about 400 pupils) were pouring out of the school and onto the playing field. The teachers came out with the registers to check that everyone was present. It was raining outside, so everyone was desperate to get back to their classrooms as quickly as possible.

Mr. Wheeler, the headmaster came out holding a large umbrella and walked over to the teachers. He said something to them which we couldn't hear and each in turn shook their head.

Mr. Wheeler came to stand in front of the gathered pupils and stared solemnly at the upturned faces. "Well done" he said. "The fire drill went very well." We all waited for him to dismiss us and send us back to the classroom but he didn't do that. Instead, he said in a loud voice "Who set off the fire alarm?" Everyone looked confused.

He told us that the prospect of a fire was a very serious business that could cost lives. He waited a while for us to digest the information and then followed it up in a loud voice with "Now, I want to know who broke the glass to set off the fire alarm? I want whoever it is to own up now." I looked at Gruffy who was grinning. I searched for Mr. Evans, who I was sure would come to our aid and explain what had happened. I caught Mr. Evans' eye. He looked at me and narrowed his eyes. The look on his face said it all. Gruffy and I were on our own. I didn't know what to do. The rain was coming down harder than ever. Most of us had come outside without our coats. There wasn't time to collect them. The headmaster was alright, he was dry because he had his umbrella.

It was then that Gruffy, with a big grin on his face, lifted his arm into the air and said "It was me and Potty Sir." (Potty being my nickname). All eyes turned to us and a big cheer went up. The headmaster was not happy. He ordered us to go to his office immediately and stand outside to wait for him. As we left our line, he was telling the school about the seriousness of false alarms before dismissing everyone back to their classrooms.

That left Gruffy and me to make our way to the headmaster's office. I was worried to death as to what would happen. We were bound to be caned. I said to Gruffy that I would tell the headmaster that Mr. Evans had told us to ring the alarm. Gruffy just smiled and said "I wouldn't bother. You'll only make it worse."

After what seemed ages, the headmaster arrived at his office, unlocked the door and said just one word "In!" We went in and stood in front of his desk, shuffling our feet.

The headmaster looked down at us both and asked us what we had to say for ourselves. I blurted out "Mr. Evans told us to do it." He looked at us in disbelief and then got really angry and lashed out at me, hitting me across the back of my head. Saying "How dare you accuse one of my staff!" Gruffy just smiled as he looked at me and said "See, I told you so."

The headmaster walked across to the corner of the room where he stored a selection of canes of various thicknesses in an old umbrella stand. He pulled out a thin cane about two feet long from the stand and turned to us "I'm going to teach you a lesson. You'll learn that it doesn't pay to let off fire alarm bells just when you feel like it. Right Pottinger, you first!"

I felt my legs go weak and was so frightened that I thought I might wet myself. I was told to put out my right hand, palm upwards. I slowly put out my hand and hoped he would change his mind but he didn't. Down came the cane across my hand. Oh, the pain! Then he asked me to lift my left hand and did the same to that hand. I felt like crying but I didn't want to do it there and then. I held it in.

The headmaster then turned to Gruffy and said "Now your turn!" I looked at Gruffy and was sure I saw a smile on his face. Gruffy also got the cane on both hands. First Gruffy grimaced but then he giggled. I couldn't believe it. Why was he laughing? The headmaster's face turned red with anger and he said "So, you think it's funny do you Foxall? Well, I'll give you something else to smile about" and caned him again on both hands.

Gruffy howled with pain and started jumping around the room holding both hands under his armpits to relieve the pain. I too was holding my hands underneath my armpits as we were told to get out of the headmaster's office.

We started to walk up the corridor still with our hands under our armpits. It seemed to ease the pain from our numb fingers. I saw a smile come across Gruffy's face and asked him what was so funny. He said "It's the fourth time I've had the cane. I think it's a record." I was speechless. Surely, he must have a screw loose or something.

Our troubles didn't end with the cane. While some of our classmates thought what we had done was very funny, others did not. Some of the fourth-year boys were out to get Gruffy and me. They weren't happy that two first year 'runts' had got them wet out there in the rain for a false fire alarm drill.

For the next couple of days, we kept our heads down. We certainly kept out of the way of the fourth-year boys but eventually they cornered us. Luckily, I was a good runner and managed to escape but poor Gruffy, with his humped back and short legs had no chance and got caught and carried into the gym. He was tied with skipping ropes to the climbing bars which were against the wall. By now a crowd of other boys had come into the gym to see what was going on.

One of the fourth-year boys said to Gruffy "You will be sentenced to Death by Tickling" and proceeded to take off Gruffy's shoes and socks. Gruffy pleaded for mercy. "No, no don't do that. I can't stand being tickled." One boy started tickling his feet while another was prodding him with a pencil. Gruffy squealed like a pig. The more they tickled him, the louder he squealed. Everyone was laughing.

Just then, the games teacher, Mr. Rogers, walked through the door to see what was the cause of all the noise which could be heard right up the corridor. He began to grin when he saw what was happening. "Okay" he said "You've had your fun. Now let him go." The boys untied him and gave him back his shoes and socks, patted Gruffy's mop of unruly black, curly hair and told him to consider himself well and truly tickled.

As Mr. Rogers left the gym, one of the fourth-year boys spotted me in the crowd and said "Right Pottinger. You're next!" I was out of that gym like a shot and kept running as fast as I could to get out of the way of those fourth formers.

I think Gruffy and me came out of the thing quite well. Half the school thought we were heroes for daring to ring the fire bell but we never did tell anyone that Mr. Evans had told us to do it. I was speechless when Gruffy admitted that he had quite liked being tickled. Like I said before, I think he definitely had a screw loose.

Chapter Eighteen

My first year at the big school soon came to an end. Apart from getting the cane, I had enjoyed it. I had made lots of new friends and I had enjoyed the various new things to which we had been introduced. I enjoyed working with my hands and so I loved the woodwork and metalwork lessons. Now that the summer holidays were here again, I was looking forward to helping with the harvest.

On the first day of the holidays, a group of boys including myself, who were aged between eleven and thirteen years old, would report to the farm manager. He would put us to work with the older workers. We would do all sorts of jobs around the farm. We would feed the pigs and the chickens and collect the eggs. We also picked potatoes and peas but the main priority was the harvest which had to be brought in. The cut corn had to be put under cover in case it got wet and was ruined.

The job I liked best was 'baling'. After the combine harvester had cut the corn, it would extract the grain and throw the excess straw out at the back. A tractor was used to pull the baler which picked up the straw and packed it tightly together. When the bale was big enough, it would be tied with string and ejected from the back of the baler. A long, wooden sledge about 7 feet x 5 feet was attached to the back of the baler and it was my job to collect the straw bales and stack them on the sledge. When the sledge was full, I would ram an iron bar into a slot in the middle of the sledge until it hit the ground and this would force the bales off the sledge. Then I had to remove the bar as soon as the last bale hit the ground.

If you got it wrong, the iron bar would smash into you and knock you off the sledge. I soon learnt to get it right.

I loved working with the older men. I felt very grown up. They would tease us if we got it wrong and would laugh at us if we stacked the bales too high and they fell on top of us. If the sun stayed out and there was no dew, we would sometimes work until it was nearly dark. We didn't mind. Especially when the farm manager would bring out flagons of cider and sandwiches for the older men and squash and cakes for us kids.

We loved Friday afternoons. It was pay day. The manager would bring out a box of brown envelopes which he would give out to the men. I felt very proud when he gave me my pay packet. On the front was written 'Young Potty' and underneath the amount I had earned (£2). We felt like millionaires.

I went home and proudly showed my wage packet to my mum. "Well done" she said but she warned me not to show it to my dad because he would want to borrow some money to take down to the pub.

The nearest town to us was Bishops Stortford which was about ten miles away. On a Saturday, a double-decker bus would come through the village twice a day. One in the morning and one in the afternoon. This was so that people could go into town to do their shopping and then return on the afternoon bus. There was also a 'late return' bus for those who wanted to go to the cinema in the town.

Now that we were rich, my friends and I would catch the afternoon bus to 'Stortford'. It would be heaving with people. When we got into town, we would wander around the shops, looking for something to buy with our hard-earned cash. I bought a new torch and some catapult elastic. At teatime, we would buy fish and chips served up in newspaper. We would put salt and lashings of vinegar on them and then find somewhere to sit and tuck in. The chips cost 4d (2½p) and the fish 9d (4p).

When we'd finished the fish and chips, we made our way to the picture house to watch a film. On a Saturday afternoon and evening there was always a queue to get in. The films were shown on a continuous reel. Sometimes, you would go in before the end of the main film and see the end first. We didn't mind. We just wanted to get in to see the films. The cheap seats cost 1s 6d (7½p).

When the last film was shown, we had to rush to the bus station to get the last bus home but before you could leave your seats in the picture house, you had to stand for 'God Save The Queen'. If you tried to sneak out before the anthem was finished, one of the staff on duty would cuff you around the ear.

The last bus home was always great fun. It was an old double-decker which was packed with kids and grown-ups pouring out of the picture house. Us kids would sit two to a seat and go over the films we'd seen. The older boys would have their girlfriends sat on their laps, chattering away and the lads who had been drinking in the pubs would be singing merrily. Not always in tune. The bus would start off and soon leave the town behind, heading for the outlying villages. Sometimes, the swaying of the bus as it went around the country lanes, would make the lads who'd been drinking feel sick. The bus conductor, a big, jolly man called Ted, would pull them up from their seats and escort them to the back of the bus and onto the platform which was open to the elements. They could then hang on to the bar on the platform and lean out of the bus to be sick.

The old bus would make its way around the villages, dropping off the passengers at their stops. By the time we got to Brent Pelham, it would be around midnight and there would only be a few of us left on the bus. Some of us would be fast asleep. Ted, who knew us, would wake us and tell us when it was time to get off the bus. When the lights and sound of the bus had faded away, we had to find our way home. If the sky was cloudy, it was pitch dark. You couldn't see your hand in front of your face. I usually had to feel for the grass verge with my feet to make sure I didn't fall in the road but now I had my new torch. If my brother Gerald was with me on the bus, he would hold onto my shoulder and we'd find our way home by the light of my torch. Mum would leave the porch light on so that we could see our way into the house. Then when we got inside, mum would be waiting for us with a cup of hot cocoa. She wouldn't go to bed until she knew we were home safe and sound.

It was about this time that my eldest brother John came home from the army. We were all very pleased and excited to see him, especially Sheila. She had waited for him for three years. The only down side was that John had to share the attic bedroom with myself and Gerald, and this caused a bit of friction. After three years in the army, John was used to tidiness and giving orders. One Friday night, John told Gerald to empty the chamber pot which was kept under one of the beds. To empty it, you had to go down two flights of stairs to the toilet. Gerald didn't want to go all that way down the stairs, so he opened the bedroom window and threw the contents out into the dark night. On Friday nights dad went to the pub and was always drunk when he came home. He had the misfortune to come home just at the time that Gerald emptied the chamber pot out of the bedroom window. We heard him shout "Bloody Hell!" We looked at each other open-mouthed. John started shouting at Gerald and I ran downstairs to tell dad that it wasn't me that had done it.

We all got downstairs just as dad came staggering drunkenly through the back door. He was soaking wet and the fag in his mouth was soggy and drooping. Mum looked at dad and said "Oh, is it raining?" "It wasn't when I left the pub" he said. "Come on" said mum "Let's take off your wet coat." "Ugh" mum said "You smell terrible. Have you been falling over in the pub toilet again?" John, Gerald and I looked at each other and started to laugh. Dad became annoyed and shouted at us to stop laughing and get to bed. That night me and my brothers laughed ourselves to sleep.

Chapter Nineteen

The school holidays were coming to an end and we had to think about going back to school.

Going back to school meant that it was a busy time for me. I still had to get out of bed before 6.30 to milk my goat, Bess. I also had a job as a paperboy. A newsagent from Buntingford wanted to start delivering papers to our village, so I applied for the job. I delivered papers to the north side of the church and a friend of mine delivered them to the south side. I had twenty-one customers on my round and delivered the papers six days a week. Pay day was on a Saturday. My wage was six shillings (30p) a week. After delivering the papers on weekdays, I had to catch the 8.15 school bus.

When I got home from school, mum would give me a list of things she needed from the village shop. When I came back with the shopping, I had to milk Bess again. This had to be done twice a day otherwise Bess would be in pain because of her swollen milk bags. No wonder she was glad to see me.

Having to milk Bess first thing in the morning before my paper round was hard when I'd only just woken up, especially on cold mornings when I didn't want to get out of bed but sometimes hard work pays off.

One morning while I was delivering the papers, one of my lady customers stopped me and asked me if it was true that I owned a goat. When I told her that it was true, she asked me if I would sell her some of the milk. She told me that it was good for the complexion and that she would pay me one shilling (5p) for a jug of milk every day. That made me very happy thinking of how I would spend this windfall.

It wasn't long before other people had heard about me selling goat's milk and they were willing to pay me for it. Bess could produce three jugs of milk a day which wasn't enough to satisfy the demand. I got greedy.

Near the kennel yard was a dairy farm where you could take your billycan and fill it up for free. I started using the cow's milk to make up the shortfall in demand. For a couple of weeks, it was a great little earner but it didn't last for long. The dairyman soon realised what was going on and chased me out of the dairy before I could fill my can. I also got a clip around the ear from the ladies that I'd tried to fool. Ah well, it was good while it lasted.

I was looking forward to going back to school after the summer holidays. I would be moving up to the second year and that meant a bit more status. The school would be having a new influx of first year pupils (runts). I was now in class 2A. There were about forty pupils in our class. We sat two to a desk and each desk had a hinged lid with a storage space underneath where we kept our books, pens and pencils. I sat next to my friend Gruffy. I had vowed never to have anything to do with him after the trouble he got me into last term but he had such an infectious smile that I couldn't resist being friends with him. I just couldn't be mad at him for long. In spite of all his mischievous ways, he was intelligent and a great help to me with my lessons.

We had only been back at school for a week when Gruffy was up to mischief again. He was sat at his desk with that wicked smile on his face. I looked at him and said "What are you up to?" "Just wait and see" he said. A few minutes later, one of the girls let out a loud scream which made everyone jump and look up from their work. Our form teacher, Miss James, looked up and said "What's the matter?" The girl had jumped up and stood away from her desk shouting "There's a mouse in my desk!" On hearing the word 'mouse', the other girls started to scream and run to the front of the class. The rest of us burst out laughing and looked at Gruffy. We knew who was responsible.

Miss James was not laughing. She'd guessed who had put the mouse there. Taking a large book from her desk, she marched up to our desk and started to hit Gruffy across the head with the book. The problem was, he was against the wall and she had to reach him by leaning across me. Now Miss James was a large-bosomed lady so that when she hit Gruffy, my head was forced into her cleavage which caused uproar amongst the boys in the class. Eventually order was restored and we were then asked to look for the mouse but we never did find it.

I enjoyed my second year at Buntingford School. I think the teachers knew that most of us were not very bright academically and pushed us towards doing practical subjects instead, like woodwork and metalwork. I had one friend who was hopeless at reading but he could repair a tractor. We were kept in line with a clip across the ear. One teacher, Mr. Clarke, kept a chastiser. It was made of a strip of leather about a foot long and two inches wide with a wooden handle fixed to one end. He kept it on his desk at the front of the class. I don't remember anyone being hit with it. I think it was the threat of him using it which kept order in the class. Mr. Clarke's subject was history and he made the lessons interesting and exciting. When he talked about battles, he would go into details so that you had a picture in your mind of what took place. He also told us about his time in the RAF as a spitfire pilot in the Second World War.

Gardening lessons were always great fun. The school had extensive gardens for growing all kinds of flowers and vegetables. The school also kept some pigs and chickens. The gardening teacher, Mr. Burge, was a very serious man. He had no sense of humour. One day he instructed me and my friend to clear a patch of tomato plants which were past their best. The friend was called John Calder and had the nickname of Monkey (Monk for short) because when he stood upright, his hands would reach his knees. It wasn't long before Monk and I got bored and started throwing the rotten tomatoes at the other boys in the garden. One of the tomatoes unfortunately hit Mr. Burge who was not amused. He rushed across the garden towards us and grabbed Monk and me by the hair, forcing us down on our knees. "Right you pair of morons, you can finish clearing the garden on your knees and if I see you standing up, I'll give you a good slapping."

Monk had an older brother whose name was Clive. They looked alike but Clive loved gardening and any spare time was spent in the garden helping the teacher. Me and Monk were on our knees pulling up tomato plants, when Clive came unseen into the garden to ask if he could help. Mr. Burge immediately grabbed him and with bulging eyes started to slap Clive around the head. "I told you that if you stood up I'd give you a slap…" and before Mr. Burge could finish his sentence, he recognised that the boy wasn't Monk at all, it was Clive.

He had hit the wrong brother. Clive reeled backwards, looking shocked. Mr. Burge, feeling full of remorse for what he'd done started to ask for forgiveness. "Oh Clive, I'm so sorry please forgive me. I thought you were that ignorant brother of yours." Poor Clive was staggering around the garden wondering what had happened to him. Monk and I were on our knees roaring with laughter.

On hearing us laughing, Mr. Burge flew into a rage and picking up a stick, rushed at us and started hitting us with it. "So, you think it's funny, do you?" and he gave us a few more whacks of the stick, before throwing it on the ground and walking back to Clive who was now stood propped against a wall looking dazed. Mr. Burge put his arm around Clive's shoulder and led him away still muttering "I'm so sorry Clive. I'll make it up to you." Monk and I looked at each other and burst out laughing.

It was about three weeks later that Monk and I got banned from the garden over an incident with the pigs. A local farmer had loaned the school four little pigs so that we could learn how to look after them. They were quite small. Only about 18 inches long and about 10 inches tall but they were very fast on their feet. They were kept in a wooden shed with straw laid down for them to sleep on. Next to the shed was a pen for the pigs to run around. These pigs were very popular but they smelt awful. Mr. Burge gave Monk and I the job of mucking them out which gave him great delight after we had played him up in the garden.

Now, pigs don't like being touched or tickled. It makes them squeal. So, when we were mucking out the pig pen, we chased the pigs around the pen and when we caught one, we'd tickle it and make it squeal. This made us laugh. Sometimes, Monk would hold one while I tickled it and the pig would squeal even louder.

There were lots of boys working in the garden at this time and, when they heard the commotion, they cheered and encouraged us to do it all the more. All this squealing and shouting soon caught the attention of Mr. Burge who angrily walked over to the pig pen to see what was going on. He caught my eye as he walked towards us, so I alerted Monk and we scarpered before he reached us. In our haste to get away, we had left the door open to the pig pen and the pigs followed us out into the garden.

The next hour was bedlam. Everyone was running around trying to catch the pigs who were squealing loudly when they were caught. The main school building overlooked the garden and it wasn't long before the other kids were leaning out of the windows cheering us on. We were having such a good laugh that if we did catch a pig, we would let it go again. In the process, we were ruining Mr. Burge's well laid out garden. He was jumping up and down with rage and shouting "Bloody hooligans!"

Eventually after much shouting and squealing, the pigs were returned to their pen. Now we had to face Mr. Burge. "Right" he said "Off to the potting shed with you two." We wondered just what he had in mind and were worried. When we got inside he told us to get a bucket of water with a brush and start cleaning the pots, ready to be used again. There were loads of them. It would take forever. He said "And if I see you slacking, you'll get a good slap."

We weren't allowed near the pigs again.

Chapter Twenty

In winter, there wasn't a lot for us to do on the farm. It was a time for ploughing and replanting the fields again and the men could cope without our help.

There were other things for us to do. The hunting and shooting season was about to begin. I liked this season. I would go up to the big house with my friends and the gamekeeper would give us our instructions as 'beaters'. We would be taken to the start point on a trailer which was pulled by a tractor.

Usually the start point would be at the far end of the wood. We would be instructed to spread out along the edge of the wood and then wait for the signal to walk into the wood hollering and beating the undergrowth with our sticks. The idea was to make the pheasants and partridges run or fly forwards. At the other end of the wood, the men with the guns would be waiting for them. These were the 'posh' people who would pay lots of money for the privilege to shoot game.

The guns were really loud when they were fired and the shot birds would be falling everywhere. That's when the gamekeeper's retriever dogs would be released to pick up the game. They would be running here, there and everywhere.

When no-one was looking, I would pick up a dead pheasant and hide it up a tree or down an old rabbit hole so that I could pick it up later. After all the birds had been retrieved, everyone would move to another wood nearby and it would start all over again.

I loved it when lunchtime arrived. Food and drink would be brought out to us from the big house. It would be laid out on two flat-top trailers. One for the posh people and one for the beaters. The posh people would have sandwiches made of all sorts of meats with tomatoes and cucumber, all washed down by champagne. We would have bread and cheese with pickled onions followed by lemonade for us and beer for the men.

After lunch, we would go out again to do some more beating. At the end of the day, we were taken by tractor and trailer back to the big house, where we would be paid for our services. I would be paid five shillings (25p) and if the day had gone well, the beaters would be given a pheasant to take home. If I was lucky, the posh people would give me a tip of a shilling (5p). On the way back home, I would go back to retrieve the pheasant I'd got stashed away.

When I got home, mum would take the pheasants, gut them and hang them on the back of the kitchen door to dry out. After a couple of days, I would help mum to pluck them and make them ready for the pot. All the family loved roast pheasant.

The gamekeeper's job was to rear and look after the pheasants and get them ready for the shooting party. If he caught you poaching his pheasants, you'd be in serious trouble with the landowner.

At this time, I would go out into the fields with my friend Roger Bennett, to make catapults. A catapult is a forked stick about eight inches long. At the top of each fork we would tie two lengths of elastic about 10" long. These lengths would then be attached to a piece of leather, to act as a pouch. In the pouch we would place a stone, ready to shoot. For the pouch, I'd use the tongue of an old shoe. Roger and I became crack shots with a catapult. We could hit a tin can on a post from 15 yards or more.

Just before it got dark, we would make our way to some quiet woodland and conceal ourselves in the trees. We had to stay very still and make no movements at all. At this time, the pheasants would come into the wood to roost and, when they were within range, we would shoot them with our catapults which we called our silent killer. On a good night, we might 'bag' two pheasants each.

By the time we left the wood it would be dark and it was easy to make our way home across the fields without being seen. When I got home, mum and dad would make out that they were angry with me for poaching. Dad said he'd get the sack if I was caught but all thoughts of getting caught were forgotten when mum produced a lovely roast pheasant for dinner.

Wintertime was the hunting season. The Puckeridge Hunt would meet at various farms and estates twice a week. The main Meet of the year would be the Christmas Meet on Boxing Day which was held at the manor house in the centre of the village. Lots of people would turn up to see the spectacle.

There would be about two hundred horses and riders taking part. The male and female riders would be smartly turned out in their black hats, black coats, white riding breeches and long black boots. Glasses of sherry on trays would be handed out to the riders which had been brought out from the big house by servants. Some riders would dismount and ask me to hold their horse while they went into the house for more 'liquid refreshment'. They would then reappear later quite merry. It would be really funny to watch them trying to mount their horses. Sometimes they would give me a shilling for holding the horse.

It was always exciting to watch the hounds appear on the scene. My friend Maddie's dad, who was the huntsman, would join us, assisted by my dad, who was the 'whipper-in'. He was there to keep the hounds together in a pack. My dad looked very smart in his red coat and white breeches.

When it was time for the hunt to move off, the huntsman would give a loud blast on his hunting horn and then move forward, followed by the field of horses and riders. Behind them would be the spectators following the hunt on foot. The riders moved on to the woodland where the fox was known to be hiding and use the hounds to rout out the fox and make him break cover. The huntsman would blow his horn which was a signal for the hounds and the field of horses to give chase. It was a wonderful sight to see the hounds racing across the fields in pursuit of the fox with two hundred horses and riders in hot pursuit.

My dad previously had told me where the hunt would take place and in which direction the fox would break cover. I could then move on to that area and wait by the field gate, ready for the horses and riders to come past. Most of them would jump the fences and gates but there were some who were either unable to do this or afraid to do so. For the latter, I would open the gate for them to gallop through. As a form of thanks, and because it was Christmas, some of the riders would throw me a sixpence or a shilling when they had gone through. Sometimes, I had to retrieve the coins from the mud.

One time, as I was doing this, a straggler came riding up to the gate but the horse refused to jump and turned away, causing the man on its back to become unseated and nearly fall off. The man's face went red with rage and he started to hit the horse with his riding crop. He looked across at me and shouted "Open that bloody gate!" I rushed to open the gate but fell in the mud just as the rider had started to gallop towards me. I had let go of the gate and it slammed shut again. The horse skidded to a halt, flinging the man from the saddle and into the gate, straight into the mud. I was nearly trampled on by the fleeing horse.

By this time, the man had got to his feet and was red-faced and angry shouting "You little hooligan. You did that on purpose." I didn't hang around to argue and was up and away across the fields. When I got to the edge of the field I turned around to see the man running around trying to catch his horse.

My dad had a wonderful affinity with animals. He had a way of getting the best out of dogs and horses. I loved to watch him go into a field of horses and just stand there. After a while, the horses would look up, see him and without any encouragement, walk over to where dad was standing and start to nuzzle him. Dad would pet them, stroke them and talk soothingly. It was the same with dogs. They all loved him. Dad put it down to 'just getting their trust'.

I saw this once, one day when my little dog Titch was unwell. Titch had developed a lump in his throat which was affecting his breathing. I was worried and asked dad if he could have a look at it. He felt along Titch's neck, looked up at me and said "I think it's some kind of a cyst." I asked if it was dangerous but he said "Only if it grows and then it could choke him to death."

I was really worried and asked dad if he could do something about it. He felt Titch's throat again and said "I think there's something I could do to help him. Go and get your mum's sewing basket." While I went to get the basket, dad went into the bathroom and came out with a razor blade.

He picked Titch up and sat him on the kitchen table. The dog looked bewildered and looked to my dad for reassurance. Dad stroked his head and talked softly to him. He took a pair of scissors from the basket and, lifting Titch's head up, he cut the fur away from around the lump. When this was done he picked up the razor blade and again, stroking and talking softly, he said to Titch as he lifted the dog's head "You must stay very still". I swear Titch understood what dad was telling him and he never moved. Dad used the razor blade to make a cut in Titch's neck about 1½ inches long, just above the lump.

The dog never took his eyes off dad. "Right little fellow" dad said "Let's see if we can get this lump out." He gently felt around the lump and gave it a squeeze. The lump just seemed to jump out. I was amazed. Dad cut away any loose ends and showed me the lump. It was a yellow colour and about the size of a chicken's egg.

Dad told me to get some hot water in a bowl and he used it to clean the wound on Titch's neck. Dad looked in mum's sewing basket and found a curved needle and some thread. He asked me to hold the skin on either side of the wound and pull the skin together.

Then dad spoke softly to Titch as he put in three stitches and sewed the sides of the wound together. The dog never moved once. Dad finished off by putting lots of Vaseline around the wound. He told me that it was my job to wash the wound every day with hot water to keep it clean.

After three days, dad took the stitches out. The whole family helped to look after Titch, spoiling him. He loved it.

When people in the village learned what dad had done and asked him how he had got the dog to sit still, dad just said "Because I asked him to." Titch went on to live to the ripe old age of fifteen years.

Chapter Twenty-One

When my brother John left the army, he got a job as a carpenter on a building site in a town called Harlow. After he'd worked there for a while, John got Gerald a job there as well. To get there, they had to cycle three miles to a village called Hare Street and from there they could catch the builders' lorry to take them the rest of the way. They were really tired by the time they got home after work but they didn't really mind the hard work. They could earn more doing this work than working on a farm.

By the late 1950s things started to change in the countryside. The young people didn't want to work on the farms, working long days for low pay. They looked further afield for employment.

We started to see the occasional car and motorbikes in the village. One of Gerald's friends had a job as an apprentice motor mechanic. My friend Gruffy's brother went off to work as a redcoat at a Butlin's Holiday Camp at Clacton-on-Sea.

When I was thirteen, mum said that I must start thinking about what I would like to do when I left school. I'd never given it a thought before. Leaving school always seemed a long way off.

I told mum I'd be happy working with the foxhounds like dad or driving a tractor on a farm. Mum gave me a look and said "No, you must learn a trade like John." She told me that living and working on a farm had lots of drawbacks. One was living in a 'tied' cottage.

The cottage belonged to the farm estate and because we didn't pay rent, we had no rights. This meant that you could be evicted at any time, just on the whim of your employer. She said that if I learnt a trade, I would not only earn more money than farm work but when I was ready to have a home of my own, I would earn enough money to pay rent, which meant I couldn't be evicted. From that time, I was determined to heed her advice.

In the spring of 1956, John and Sheila decided to get married. We were all delighted and never more so when at the end of the following year they had a son. They named him Kevin.

After a while, John and Sheila wanted to move back to Poulton in Gloucestershire, where most of our family lived. John had found a cottage to rent and a job as a carpenter. We were sorry to see them leave but mum said it was time for them to find their own way in life.

When they left, mum told Gerald that he could have a bedroom of his own. In all my life, I had never had a bedroom all to myself. It would take some getting used to. I missed the company of my brother Gerald. It was so quiet but after a while I started to like my own company and it meant that I had more time to read my history books.

Chapter Twenty-Two

It was a good time for me when I moved up to the third year at school. I started to see things differently. I started to enjoy maths, history and woodwork. The teachers who taught these subjects made them really interesting and fun. I was never any good at English because the teacher had no patience with us. You couldn't ask her any questions. If you did, she would angrily tell us to look it up and find out for ourselves which wasn't always possible. You learnt not to ask questions.

I started to do well on the sports field. I was chosen to represent the school in track and cross-country races. I won the one-mile race when I was thirteen. What I loved most was football. However, I wasn't quite good enough to play for the school but I was picked for the cricket team. My friend Monk would always get picked as bowler because, although he wasn't very tall and had short legs, he had abnormally long arms. When he stood up, his arms would reach his knees. He was the fastest bowler in the school. It made me smile to watch the batsman's face when he saw that Monk was bowling and when our wicket-keeper moved back about five yards.

Our games teacher, Mr. Rogers, started a boxing club. It proved to be very popular. We were taught how to protect ourselves and how to counter punch. Boxing made me feel more confident and able to deal with any difficult situations.

However, storm clouds were gathering on the horizon. I came home one day to find my dad sat in the kitchen. He was writing a letter at the kitchen table. This seemed strange. I'd never seen dad writing a letter before. If there were any letters to write, mum would always write them.

I asked dad about the letter but he told me to mind my own business. Mum was working at the sink so I asked her about the letter and she told me that dad was applying for another job. My heart sank. "Does this mean that we'll be shiftin' again?" I asked her. Mum smiled and told me that he probably wouldn't get the job anyway.

This didn't really make me feel any better. I was worried about moving again. I liked living here and had made lots of friends and was doing well at school. I went back over to dad and asked him why he wanted to leave his job but he told me it would mean promotion and more money coming into the house. He finished writing the letter, put it in an envelope and asked me to take it into the village and post it.

On the way to the post box, I looked at the address and saw that it was addressed to someone in Horningsea near Cambridge which was about thirty miles away. I had thoughts on destroying the letter but I just couldn't do it. That would be wrong so I reluctantly put it into the post box.

Two weeks later dad had a reply to his letter. He was invited to go for an interview. Dad had applied for the job of head groom to a Showjumping family and a house came with the job.

For the first time ever, mum insisted on looking at the house before he took the job, so she went with him to the interview. Mum said that if the house wasn't good enough for us to live in, then we weren't moving. Arrangements were made for them to go to Horningsea and mum went with him to check over the house which was on offer. I hoped the house wasn't up to standard or that dad would fail the interview.

It was late evening when they returned home. Dad came in with a big smile on his face saying "I've got the job! We're shiftin'!" I looked at mum hoping she would say that the house was no good but she told us that it was a lovely house which you approached down a long drive lined with poplar trees on each side. This wasn't the news I wanted to hear. I was upset and so was Gerald.

Arrangements were made to leave the village in three weeks' time. I was walking round in a daze. This was all too sudden. The next three weeks were awful. I had to arrange for another boy to take over my paper round. I hated having to tell my friends at school. My teachers wished me luck and my sports teacher tried to cheer me up by saying that there were great sporting facilities in Cambridge.

I felt terrible when I had to say goodbye to my village friends. Especially Maddie next door. She'd been such a good friend to me and shown me how to milk the goat. I was almost in tears saying goodbye to my friend Gruffy. He'd got me into trouble many times but I still thought the world of him.

Gerald didn't want to 'shift' this time. He was happy working as a trainee bricklayer. He also had a lovely girlfriend called Pam. A family friend, Mrs. Bennett, offered for Gerald to lodge at her house but mum persuaded him to come with us.

Brent Pelham was a friendly village and everyone knew each other. When I called on my friends, I was always invited inside. My friends loved to come to my house too because they were always welcomed in by mum who would serve up tea and homemade cake but this would all change with our next move.

It was spring of 1958 when we left Brent Pelham. We had lived there for three years. Longer than we had lived anywhere else. I really hoped that something would stop us moving but it never did. We all helped to load up the removals lorry and when we'd finished, we took a last look around the empty house. At that moment, I didn't much like my dad for making us move again. We all climbed into the lorry (which had seating for all of us) and set off for our new home.

Horningsea was thirty-five miles away from Brent Pelham and three miles from Cambridge. The area is known as The Fen Country because it's flat and wet. It took about two hours to get there. Our new house was half a mile outside the village and the driveway with the poplar trees down each side was very impressive. As we drove towards the house, we could see a group of people standing outside arguing.

Dad told us to stay in the lorry while he went to talk to them. A serious discussion was taking place. When dad came back, he was accompanied by a well-dressed lady who was looking very confused. Dad looked glum as he said "The people in our new house won't shift!" The lady told us her name was Mrs. Jacobs and she was dad's new employer. She told us she was sorry about all the confusion but would try to sort it out. She then got into her car and sped off down the drive, leaving us to sort ourselves out.

Gerald suggested going back to Brent Pelham but dad said "That's daft. Someone's taken my job there and moved into our old house." The removals men weren't happy either. They just wanted to unload our furniture and go home. Mum looked upset and dad came out with his usual statement "Don't worry! Summat'll turn up."

We all sat there looking glum and not sure what to do next when a lady appeared from inside the house. "I'm so sorry to cause all this trouble but my husband's job he'd applied for has fallen through, and as a house went with the job, we have nowhere to go." Her name, she told us, was Mrs. Foster. She offered us all a cup of tea. We couldn't believe it. We were left homeless and this lady was offering us tea.

Chairs were brought out and the two families were sat side by side drinking tea with the removals men. All we could hope for was a solution from Mrs. Jacobs, who we hoped would reappear very soon. An hour later, she came back in her car to tell us that she had a solution to our problem. She had found a house for us in the village and would take us there. We all piled back into the lorry with a heavy heart, not knowing what to expect.

Horningsea is a pretty village with a busy road running through it. There were two shops and two pubs. At first glance, I thought we might be alright living here. The houses looked attractive with well-kept gardens containing pretty flowers. Further on, we came to a square of old cottages. In the middle of the square was a brick-built wash-house for the use of all the residents of the cottages. At the back of the square was an alleyway leading to some gardens. My heart sank.

Ours was a two-up and two-down cottage. It was in an appalling state. Plaster was coming off the walls and the stone floor was breaking up. Mum was angry and turned on Mrs. Jacobs, telling her it was a dirty slum. "We can't live here" mum said. Mrs. Jacobs told us we had no choice for the time being but would look around for something better. Mum got no support from dad. He just shrugged his shoulders and announced "At least we have a roof over our heads." We all looked murderously at him as Mrs. Jacobs said "That's the spirit!" Then she left us to settle in.

The next hour felt like a nightmare. All of our possessions were unloaded and put in the house anywhere that there was a space. After the removals men had gone, we found somewhere to sit and take stock of the situation. Mum couldn't make a cup of tea because, although the house had electricity, we needed someone to wire up the electric cooker to boil a kettle.

As always, the first job was to get the beds put together. It was hard work getting the beds upstairs because the staircase was so narrow. The bedrooms were very small and when the beds were put in the rooms, there was little room for anything else. A neighbour called in and introduced himself to us. His name was Ken Bates.

Ken was really helpful. He connected the cooker so that we could make a cup of tea and cook something to eat. He showed us where the toilets were located. It was a block of seven toilets and they were around the back of the house, up an alleyway and across the gardens. They were chemical toilets which were emptied every Tuesday by the council. He left us with the passing shot "Just don't be around here on Tuesdays. The smell is awful!"

Mum and dad seemed to have a way of accepting their lot. By the end of the day they were doing their best to make this terrible place livable. Gerald and I hated the place. In a matter of hours, we had left a nice house in a nice village to come here and live in a hovel. I felt miserable but I knew I had no choice but to get used to the situation. There was no going back.

The next day, Gerald and I had a walk around the village. The main road was quite busy with traffic. This was something we weren't used to seeing but it did have a bus service into Cambridge every two hours. We were pleased and surprised to find that the River Cam ran past the village, only a few hundred yards away. There were several fishermen on the banks of the river and motor boats going by. I thought that perhaps I might like living here after all.

A week later, Gerald decided he didn't want to stay in Horningsea and wrote to Mrs. Bennett in Brent Pelham to ask if he could stay with her. In a few days, she had replied to the letter, saying that he was welcome to lodge with her but he would have to talk it over with mum and dad. He explained to them that he had left behind good friends and a good job in Brent Pelham but the deciding factor was Pam, the girl he had left behind.

Mum tried to persuade him to stay but his mind was made up. He explained that now he was a man, he would have to stand on his own two feet and make his own decisions. I was sad to see Gerald leave home. We were not only brothers, we were good friends and he could always make me laugh. I longed to go with him but knew it just wasn't possible.

Over the next few weeks, I did my best to settle in but I found it hard to get to know people. They were reserved and kept themselves to themselves. I was never asked to go inside their houses. Some were shocked when I told them that I lived in the square. Someone said that the square was due to be demolished and that only homeless people were sent there by the council.

Living at 'The Square' was not easy. The cottage was in a terrible condition: the window frames and the stairs were rotten, plaster was falling off the walls and it was a fifty-yard walk up the garden to go to the toilet.

For the first time, it was a joy when dad came in one day and announced "We're shiftin'!" Mum looked at me before turning to dad saying "Have you got the sack already?" Dad smiled and said "No, we've got a better house and it's just down the road."

The new house was about 150 yards down the high street. It was semi-detached with dormer bedrooms in the roof. There was a large living room and just off this room was the kitchen which had a 'range' fireplace. One of the rooms had been turned into a bathroom with a toilet. From the hallway, a staircase led up to two large bedrooms in the roof space. Mum said that she thought she could make it very cosy and said she was pleased with the large garden.

The next day, dad borrowed a van and with the help of two of our neighbours, we moved everything from the house in 'The Square'. Mum said "At last we won't have to go up the garden to go to the toilet." I gave a cheer and there were smiles all round. This was a good move.

Moving to a better house made me feel better about living in Horningsea. Dad seemed to like his new job and mum was happy because she could go into Cambridge for her bible reading.

Chapter Twenty-Three

It was now time to enrol at a new school. I wasn't keen to start at another new school but mum said that I had no choice. I had to go to school and that was that. There was a bus that collected schoolchildren from the village to take them to Bottisham College in Bottisham. Mum thought it sounded very posh.

The next day I dressed ready for school and waited at the bus stop. There was quite a crowd of children waiting there already. They wanted to know my name and where I'd lived before coming to Horningsea. The school was five miles away and stopped at other villages on the way, to pick up other children. I sat next to a boy from our village who said he would take me into school and show me how to get to the secretary's office.

I knocked on the door of the office and a lovely smiley lady opened the door and asked me to come in. She asked me about myself and took down all the details and then escorted me to my classroom to introduce me to my teacher. As we entered the classroom, the other children looked up from their work to stare at me. There were about thirty-five children in the class.

I was introduced to my new form teacher, Miss Robertson. "Welcome" she said. "Come in and tell us all about yourself." I was so embarrassed to be the centre of attention with all those eyes looking at me. There was silence while everyone waited for me to say something. Then I took courage, mumbled my name and said that I lived in Horningsea. My family had moved there because my father had got a promotion and a new job in the area. Luckily, they didn't press me for more details.

I did my best to settle in. Nobody was unkind to me but I always felt isolated. Within the class, friendships and groups of children were formed to help each other. I felt embarrassed to ask questions. I found myself trying to work things out myself and was always playing 'catch up'.

I performed much better on the playing field. The main sport which the school played was cricket. I found that I was better than most and always asked to play as part of a team. In the lunch breaks, there was always a game being played on the school field. The rules were very simple: if you wanted to bat, you had to bowl or catch the batsman out. It was great fun. There were always lots of eager lads fielding and waiting for a catch, and others lining up waiting to bowl.

One day when I joined the game, I noticed the lad who had come in to bat, was hitting the ball very easily. This was because the bowlers were bowling the ball very slowly. I asked one of the lads why the bowler didn't bowl the ball faster. He told me that the batsman was called Bartley and he was a bit of a bully and anyone that bowled him out would get a 'thumping'.

I didn't take this threat seriously. When it was my turn to bowl the ball, I took a long run up to the wicket and bowled the ball as fast as I could at Bartley. The ball hit the ground in front of him, bounced up and struck him in the ribs, causing him to step backwards onto his wicket, knocking it down. Everyone shouted "Out!" Bartley tried to protest but to no avail. He was out.

Bartley went red with rage and threw his bat to the ground. As he walked off the field, he pointed at me and said "I will get you for this!"

For the rest of the day, I thought it would be wise to keep out of Bartley's way until his temper subsided but it didn't. He caught up with me in the locker room where I was getting my books for the afternoon lessons.

I was trapped and had nowhere to run. I tried to reason with him but he just smirked and pushed me backwards. My heart started to pound as he pushed me again.

Then something happened: I began to feel angry. Bartley put his hand up to push me again. He looked surprised when I pushed his hand away with my left hand and punched him on his nose with my right hand, causing him to stumble backwards. He held his nose and was shocked to find that it had started to bleed.

I braced myself for the expected onslaught but it never came. Bartley glared at me while still holding his nose. He turned and, much to my relief, he ran from the room.

Later that day, I was called into the headmaster's office. He asked me to explain my behaviour in the locker room. I tried to explain but the headmaster cut me short and said "I have spoken to Bartley and he said that you attacked him." Again, I tried to explain but he just wasn't interested in my side of the story and told me that he wouldn't tolerate fighting in this school, and that I must learn to turn and walk away.

I came out of his office seething with anger. I remembered the time many years ago when I was at Siddington School and was punished for attacking the boy who was the school bully, when really, he had set on me. It had happened again. I was fed up with school.

Chapter Twenty-Four

Our neighbours next door were Mr. and Mrs. Butler. They had a son about the same age as me called Walter but everyone called him Wally. He was a bit of a loner but he was always friendly to me. He didn't often go to school and told me that he'd rather go fishing which seemed fair enough to me. Many a time I would go with him.

The River Cam was only a couple of fields away from where we lived and it was a great river for fishing. The river was about fifteen metres wide and, on our side of the river, were little inlets where people would moor their small boats.

Wally had a two-man canoe and he taught me how to paddle and how to fish. One day, we skived off school and took his canoe all the way to Cambridge about three miles away. I loved it. It gave me such a sense of freedom.

The river ran right through the centre of the city and passed by some of the famous colleges. The one I liked the best was Kings College. It had lovely lawns that ran down to the river and the students would be boating on punts using long poles to move along.

I started going into Cambridge more often. I was fascinated by city life and loved to walk through the parks and look at the world-famous university. There were lots of red buses to get around the city and I learnt to dodge paying the fare by telling the bus conductor that I'd got on the wrong bus.

I started to go to school less often. I'd worked out that I only needed to go for another four weeks because when the new school term started in September I would be fifteen. This meant that I was old enough to go to work.

I daren't tell mum that I was taking time off school. She would have gone mad. Instead of catching the school bus, I would sneak off to the river and follow the towpath all the way into Cambridge where I would explore the city. I spent hours in the museums there.

The place that really fascinated me was the outdoor market where the stallholders would be selling their wares by shouting out their patter to encourage the people to buy. In the centre of the market was a wooden tea shack which was run by an elderly couple: Alf and Bett. They sold bacon and cheese butties to everyone including the other stallholders.

It was a great place for a good gossip. I got talking to Alf one day when I went to buy a mug of tea. The cost of the tea was thruppence but I only had tuppence in my pocket so I suggested to Alf that if I didn't have milk in my tea, could I pay him tuppence? Alf realised that this was probably all I had and smiled saying "tuppence it is then".

I sat down on a nearby bench and drank my tea, thinking what a nice man he was, and wondered if I could do something for him to repay him for his kindness to me. I noticed that there were a lot of empty mugs scattered around. When I'd finished my tea, I collected all the empty mugs and took them back to the shack. Alf's wife Bett smiled and said "How would you like a little job on

Saturdays? We can pay you five shillings plus bacon butties and tea." I jumped at the offer.

The market was always busy on Saturdays. The stallholders didn't always want to leave their stalls to get their tea and butties, so I offered to get them for them.

One day Alf asked me if I could count. When I nodded, he took me round the back of the shack and showed me where he kept the money. It was in an old bucket under the counter. It was full of pennies and ha'pennies.

Alf had a job for me. He wanted me to count the takings and take them to the bank. I had to count the coins and put them into little bags so that the bank would know how much we wanted to pay in at a glance. Alf told me to get counting "That'll take you an hour or two" he said.

The bucket of coins was so heavy that I struggled to lift it and staggered over to a quieter corner of the shack to count them. I had a pile of little bags on one side of me which were supplied by the bank and started counting the coins and filling the bags. In each bag, I had to put 60 pennies or 120 ha'pennies.

I sat there counting and filling the bags for over two hours. Although they didn't look it, the coins were dirty and made my hands black with grime. When Bett came to see how I was getting on, she told me that I looked like a little Fagin with those bags of coins all around me.

When I'd finished counting the coins, I wrote down the amount in each bag and then added them together to get a total amount. It came to £27 10s 0d.

Bett gave me a cup of tea and a piece of cake saying "Well done lad. We always hated doing that job." When it was time to go, Alf gave me two bags of coins and told me that one bag was my wages and the other was my bonus for doing a good job. I went home feeling as proud as punch.

Chapter Twenty-Five

Although I was enjoying my little adventures into Cambridge and my fishing trips with Wally, I felt a little lonely. I made friends easily but had this feeling of not belonging anywhere. In fact, I felt this way every time I moved house. My new friends would talk about their brothers, sisters, aunts and uncles who lived nearby. They belonged, but I was just passing through.

My dad seemed happy in his new job but for how long? Mum was happy living near Cambridge so that she could attend her bible readings. She asked me to go with her but I would rather go fishing.

My school days were coming to an end. I began to think about what I would like to do when I left school. If I was still living in Brent Pelham, I would probably be working on the farm or perhaps with my brother on the building site. Here, I didn't know who would employ me. I thought about what dad would say: "Don't worry. Summat'll turn up."

On my next day at school, I was told an appointment had been made for me to see the Careers' Officer. Maybe that would settle the matter. His name was Mr. Stewart. I didn't really know what to expect when I walked into his office.

He beckoned to me to sit down on the other side of a large desk. He smiled at me and said "What do you want to do when you leave school?" I didn't know what to say. I hadn't really make up my mind yet. "I don't know. I haven't got a clue" I said. He looked puzzled for a while then said "Tell me about yourself. Let me get to know you."

I started to tell him about my life and how many schools I'd attended. I also told him about all the house moves and how it had made me feel. He looked amazed at what I'd told him and wanted to know more. I felt pleased that at last someone was interested in me and what I had to say. I began to tell him everything that had happened to me.

He was surprised that I had been driving tractors since I'd been aged twelve and he roared with laughter when I told him about substituting cow's milk for goat's milk so that I could sell it for more money.

When I had finished my story, he said "Richard, you have had a lot of disruption in your short life but don't let that make you a failure. Make it a strength. You have no qualifications on paper but you have many life experiences to draw on. You are friendly and show a willingness to work. I think I can find you a job. Go away now and enjoy your summer holidays and then come back to see me. It's time you went out and made your mark in the adult world."

I got up to leave but as I reached the door, he called me back. As I looked at him he said "Richard! Always remember that if people like you, they will help you."

I came out of his office feeling on top of the world. He had made me feel that I did belong. There was a vast adult world out there waiting for me and if I tried hard enough, I could belong to it. I was feeling happier but a little apprehensive about what life had in store for me. Whatever it was, I felt confident that I could handle whatever life could throw at me... but for now, I'm going fishing!